CHASING FOOTNOTES

LILIA J. DON

DEDICATION

to my daughters, Maia and Raia:

May you always stand strong in the knowing of who you are, embracing the truth that your identity is not fixed but a beautifully fluid journey - ever evolving, ever growing. May you confidently root yourself in this understanding while allowing room for introspection and transformation, knowing that each moment is an opportunity to become more aligned with your true self.

May you always stand up for what is right, for yourselves and for others, with a heart full of courage and a spirit fueled by bravery. Let your actions reflect the strength within you. Your thoughts are seeds, but it is through effort and intentional action that they take root and thrive. You are the creator of your own life, and by aligning your thoughts, beliefs, words and actions, you can bring your visions to life. Stand tall in this truth every single day, and always remember to be your own greatest ally. Be kind to yourself, nurture your spirit, and honour your journey with the same compassion you would offer to a dear friend. And remember, give the light of your spirit only to those who are worthy of it, for it is a gift that thrives when shared with those who cherish its warmth.

CONTENTS

1 Opening statements   Pg 1

2 Everything is energy   Pg 27

3 Peeling back the layers   Pg 45

4 A metamorphosis kind of transformation   Pg 84

5 Surrender to the flow of life   Pg 117

6 Acceptance of all as it is   Pg 133

7 There is only one way to eat an elephant: one bite at a time   Pg 152

8 Self-dialogue   Pg 167

9 Trial and refinement   Pg 183

10 Mapping your pathway, with purpose   Pg 195

11 Building lasting habits   Pg 210

12 Abundance starts from within   Pg 224

13 Don't carry what isn't yours to carry   Pg 239

14 Conclusion   Pg 250

i. Key Principles of Chasing Footnotes   Pg 252

ii. About the Author   Pg 263

iii. Acknowledgements   Pg 264

1 OPENING STATEMENTS

I come from humble beginnings, born and raised in Bulgaria, where my childhood was filled with carefree days, endless family time, laughter, and the simple, mundane joys of life, along with plenty of outdoor play. Although we lived in the city, in Ruse much of our free time was spent at my grandparents' summer villa by the Danube River or at my parents' holiday house in the mountains, in Selo Tarkasheni near Elena, in the Balkans - my maternal grandfather's birthplace. He was an exceptionally fascinating and knowledgeable man, with a background in the secret services, and he spent countless hours teaching me history, telling me stories, and even showing me how to shoot. He also taught me how to play chess and belote, and we played a lot of strategic games at home, including backgammon. My grandmother, a phenomenal artist, shared her artistic skills with me, nurturing a love for creativity and expression. We were naturally closer to my mother's side of the family. My mother had some involvement in that secret services world as well, though no further details were ever disclosed - she had sworn to secrecy and, true to her nature, honored that oath. She has promised to reveal more in her own memoirs one day, which in turn I may share in subsequent publications.

But for me, my favorite place was always the mountains. There, I could roam free. There, I could just be me. I became an expert mushroom picker - so much so that the elderly in the village still remember me for it. We fished, caught river crabs with our bare hands - we did it all. Life was raw, adventurous, and filled with nature's untamed beauty.

However, everything changed when my family emigrated to South Africa when I was in my teens. I'd say I became a rather rattled teenager, suddenly taken away from everything I had ever known and loved and thrust into a new country, where I hardly spoke the language although I did have a great understanding of it, didn't have any friends and family around, other than my immediate family, and had lost all comforts as my parents started building a life from scratch, quite literally. Every experience felt like an uphill battle, and I encountered difficulties that many wouldn't ordinarily face every step of the way, from the very moment I entered into the country. At the time I did not realise it, but I was in a downward spiral which I had no idea how to break free from, as none of the people around me had the skills or knowledge to help me. For the first time, I felt alone and as if I did not belong. Yet, I remained flexible and mingled with crowds where I did not belong me had the skills or knowledge on the topic to pass onto me. For the first time, I felt alone and as if I did not belong, yet I maintained flexibility and fit into places and mingled with crowds I did not belong with, until eventually I did find my way...

My parents were, and still are, rather mismatched as a couple primarily because they did not make the effort to integrate, each maintaining their individual worlds with minimal overlap, although they have managed to retain a level of friendship throughout the years. My mother, driven by her own fears and missteps, pushed us relentlessly to avoid the regrets she felt about her own life. She is exceptionally smart, well-read with a sharp mind that excels in academic settings but doesn't go the extra mile of application of all her acquired knowledge and battles with the emotional side of things and the nuances of human interaction, despite her very social nature. While she navigates the world with remarkable analytical skills, she has difficulty understanding others and asserting herself to pursue what she truly wants. This disconnect manifests in her communication style: she often speaks her mind without much consideration as to how her words might affect those around her, yet fails to speak up when she really should. Her well-meaning intentions can sometimes come across as harsh or insensitive, leading to misunderstandings and strained relationships. In her quest for honesty, she overlooks the importance of empathy and the art of listening and gentle delivery. This dynamic has provided me with a unique opportunity to develop the skills I considered important, such as understanding myself and people, navigating situations with empathy, and actively standing up for myself and those around me. Growing up in this environment taught me the value of communication that fosters connection, allowing me to learn how to express myself thoughtfully while remaining true to myself. I strive to create dialogue that honours both my voice and the perspectives of others, recognising that vulnerability and understanding are key to meaningful interactions.

My father on the other hand is more of a resourceful and emotionally attune man who is aware of his surroundings, can get a good feel for people, but he grapples with feelings of inadequacy and a need to constantly prove his masculinity and assert himself in an authoritative manner. His deep desire to protect us sometimes limited our freedom, as his fears clouded his judgment and led to overprotection. Ironically, my parents could have made the perfect couple, as they truly complement each other's strengths and weaknesses, had they worked together as a team. Despite their personal challenges and incompatibility, they have remained together and I was undoubtedly loved and cared for in the best way they knew how to, though my mother's constant comparisons with others often stripped me of joy and reinforced the notion that I was not good enough as I was, so I had to become more, and then some more... Naturally, there was a lot of clashing, power-struggles and resistance from my side, which in hindsight did make me stronger, more resilient and assertive.

While my father adored my mother in his unrefined ways, he was constantly undermined by my mother's inability to appreciate his qualities and accept him for who he is. This dynamic made him intolerant and impatient, struggling with the weight of feeling unrecognised and unappreciated. In a desperate bid for approval, he turned to gambling, hoping to achieve success that would finally earn my mother's respect. Perhaps his descent into gambling was partly a result of having nothing to occupy his time after being retrenched, but regardless of the actual reason behind it, had he not gone down that path, he might never have taken the steps to emigrate to South Africa. As a creature of comfort, he was generally unwilling to explore or seek adventure, and this drastic change pushed him out of his comfort zone in ways he would not have chosen on his own. Yet this pursuit only led to loss, achieving the opposite of what he desired. Instead of gaining admiration, his gambling spiralled into a source of conflict and disappointment, further complicating the dynamics in our home. Discussing this is still a sore point for him, so many years later. I am mentioning all of this on a very superficial level not with the intention to criticise my upbringing or my parents, but rather with the intention to demonstrate that we are all human and have all sorts of complex and sometimes messy backgrounds and regardless of such, we remain in control as the creators of our own realities and we can all achieve personal growth and evolution.

From a young age, I always had a very strong sense of right and wrong and preferred spending time with people much older than me, for I tended to have better conversations, and as a teenager navigating the challenges of a new environment, I didn't always make the choices I knew were right, which of course led to self-criticism, guilt, shame and the works. I spent most of my lunch breaks at school alone, hidden away from the critical eyes of others, grappling with feelings of isolation and inability to fit in with such a juvenile crowd. But I was resilient, learning to adapt and make do with whatever was in front of me, albeit I battled with accepting my new reality. I fought it hard, and when we go against the flow of life, we are really going against ourselves, but I found it exceptionally frustrating to not be in control of my own life (or so I thought at the time) and watching my parents' mistakes drove me up the wall.

Fast forward to my mid-twenties, as I journeyed toward becoming a legal professional, after several years of uncertainty post-graduation, I encountered some of the toughest men under the sun, and through these experiences, I learned to not only recognise my own worth, but to also recognise the value and perspective I added in everything I did. I always took great pride in applying myself to the best of my abilities and always strived to achieve the best results possible in my career. A bit of a perfectionist syndrome, which turns out to be the lowest standard one can adhere to. My greatest mentors in my professional journey were Emile van der Merwe, a private investigator with a military intelligence background, and Peter Horwitz, a brilliant legal mind and former chief whip of the Democratic Alliance in Gauteng, South Africa. Emile not only taught me the importance of keen observation and intuition but also helped me believe in myself and my potential to become a legal professional in the first place. He encouraged me to pursue further studies and instilled in me the courage to stand up for myself and speak up in challenging situations. He even taught me things I should probably not mention in writing should I ever encounter a dangerous situation. Just a quick note as I transitioned from one job to the other - Emile didn't want to lose me. When Peter asked him for a reference during my interview, I knew I wouldn't get the job… or so I thought. Emile told Peter, word for word, that if he hired me, he'd bomb his office and piss on his grave. Needless to say, that turned out to be the best reference I could've asked for. Peter, an equally tough and emotionally crippled man, appreciated the extent of my honesty, which was rather unrefined in my younger years - not many dared to be as blunt with him. Blunt is all I knew how to be, but I adapted and learnt as I grew. Peter taught me two invaluable lessons: never make a threat I don't intend to follow and master the art of eloquently expressing myself - especially in legalese. He believed in me unreservedly, saw my potential, and pushed me to become great. His language was as sharp as it was refined, and he had a way with words that made even the most mundane legal correspondence feel like an art form. Whenever we drafted a letter of demand, he'd say with a smirk, "This is the 'Fuck You' letter - rude letter to follow." Their guidance challenged me to embrace my strengths, trust my judgement and approach my career with both courage and authenticity.

Another person who profoundly shaped who I am today, but is no longer with us, was Maria Smith, a visionary with supernatural gifts. She guided me on a deeply personal level, teaching me how to become more perceptive and shedding the naïveté of the girl I once was. Maria taught me how to read people, how to patiently position myself as needed, and how to navigate life with greater awareness and intention. She was like a mother to me, and we chatted almost daily - sometimes for hours on end. She was one of the few people who truly knew me, understood me, and loved me for everything that I am. Her wisdom, love, and insight are gifts I carry with me, and I am forever grateful for the profound impact she had on my life.

I won't delve into the specifics of my struggles or mistakes not because of the lack thereof, but because they are actually so many and also, they do not define me – they were all paving the way to a more authentic version of me. Our true potential is unlocked through self-exploration which mostly tends to happen in the midst of difficult times, where we shed the limiting beliefs imposed by others when we uncover who we truly are at our core, our authentic self. Much like a crab or lobster that sheds its old shell to grow, we too must allow ourselves to be vulnerable in order to evolve. The discomfort of this shedding process - leaving behind the familiar and the protective layer can feel overwhelming, but it is through this vulnerability that we step into our power. Trusting the process and believing in something greater than ourselves, we allow our new, stronger selves to emerge, unburdened by the past and more aligned with who we have always been. By standing strong in that truth, unwavering in the face of the world's challenges, we can live a life of integrity, grounded in authenticity and resilience. My story is one of resilience and growth, a testament to the belief that we can carve our own paths and create lives filled with meaning, kindness and joy, regardless of our circumstances or origin. It's not the circumstances we face that truly matter, but our state of being amidst them that does.

Through my upbringing, I've learned to balance the intellectual rigor exemplified by my mother with the emotional depth and adaptability embodied by my father. This balance, along with the lessons from my grandparents - my grandfather's strength in discipline and my grandmother's wisdom in creativity has shaped my ability to trust the process, knowing that the vulnerability of shedding the old will eventually give way to the emergence of a stronger, truer version of myself. While I appreciate my parents' efforts to do what they thought was best, I recognise that they lived much of their lives unaware of their true power and infinite potential and naturally, I ended up adopting a lot of their own ways and struggles, along with their favourable qualities too. Their journeys have highlighted the importance of self-discovery, understanding that you cannot pass on knowledge you don't possess yourself and that you need not carry the burdens of others. I strive to honour their experiences while forging my own path - one that values understanding, compassion, and the strength found in vulnerability. Ironically, that's where your strength lies, when you dare to honour your authentic self, regardless of the opinions and judgements of others. There's always been and there will always be those people who will do just that, try to stomp all over you to make themselves feel more powerful and important, but even that comes with a lesson if you let it be one. You will be tested time and time again and it is up to you to firmly hold your ground, regardless of who is trying to shake things up under your feet and regardless of the . severity thereof. Literally everything and everyone can be your teacher and it's up to you to recognise it, implement it and live your life according to your own beliefs and those can be adjusted at any point in time.

This book is not about me per se, although I think it's important for you to know a little bit about me and more particularly about snippets of my journey which has undoubtedly led me to where and who I am today. We all have a background, a story, and it's not always pretty. I will try not to bore you with too many personal anecdotes, unless I am trying to drive a specific point by means of examples extracted from my personal life and I shall try to keep it as concise and as flowing as can be.

Being the typical lawyer that I am, I'll add my little disclaimer - I am not trying to make any claims of groundbreaking methodologies or ideas you've never encountered or thought of before and I do encourage you to tap into your own higher self and inner wisdom and take my words to an elevated level. I totally encourage that. Any repetitions are purposeful, so they may be reaffirmed and hopefully, stick for good. If you see spelling errors, those are purposeful too, from a copyright perspective. My sole aim is to share the insights and experiences that have profoundly shaped my journey toward self-discovery and authentic way of living and I hope to offer you a fresh perspective and if that doesn't quite resonate, I am certain you'll find something slightly more pickled, whatever your preference! We always tend to take out what we are ready to receive out of anything we encounter. My goal is to awaken the parts of you that are waiting to be awakened, inviting you to explore the depths of your being and embrace your true self for this is where we want to be. Through my own journey, I have found that all the answers to any questions I have ever had, such as who am I, what is my purpose, my passions, my triggers, is this a good decision, what's happening within my body, how to better self-regulate or simply, what do I feel like eating today, all lie within me. I suppose the most important questions of them all, to me at least, is probably: who am I and how do I live a life that is representative of who I am, my beliefs, my goals whilst doing so authentically, without the anxiety of not doing enough or the guilt that I should do better every step of the way, remaining true to myself, remaining flexible in my thinking whilst rigid with the non-negotiables and truly experience the inner peacefulness and joy whilst doing so with integrity. What a mouthful, but I reckon, it flows. Remember, none of this is supposed to feel like hard work or burdensome information overload, but rather a great and exciting opportunity and journey of self-discovery and I suggest if that's not how you feel to perhaps consider reframing your perceptions even if only for purposes of going through everything that follows – it may just be worth your while, who knows? Doing something as simple as changing your own definition of the words that represent change, growth, uncertainty can literally change your whole outlook and experience of life. Anything you dare to know, you can, provided you are in tune with yourself and know how to identify the answers within, and how to dispose of the mind-clutter or inner noise that may be clouding any answers. I will discuss my thought patterns and experiences in a way that hopefully resonates with you in a practical and logical manner. My aim is to support you in awakening, improving, or developing those aspects of yourself that are ready to flourish, perhaps even beyond what you thought possible.

I don't claim to know all the answers to all of life's questions, but I do know the answers to the questions I have dared to ask insofar as I am concerned, the flow of life and you can do the same for you. I am by no means any more special than you are, but all the work I have done on myself certainly does show in the way I feel, in the way I move through life, in my attitude and interactions with others and everyone deserves to experience a similar sense of comfort in their own skin, in their own way, and live in a state of well-being and fulfilment, should they not already. Although not perfect, I do know how to find my way back to myself when I stray from my path, figuratively speaking, and let's not beat around the bush – we all do sometimes, especially when we are in the stage of growth and transition from an older version of oneself. We all make mistakes, get distracted along the way and end up doing what we are familiar with if not consciously then subconsciously (which is really our own creation too – I call this our brain's version of a wastebasket, where everything we do not know how to deal with or fear to deal with goes), and could easily revert to a cycle of past experiences and habits. We all deserve the tools to live life on our own terms, being true to ourselves and pursuing our dreams with integrity instead of feeling helpless, as if we are victims. We are not victims, ever, and don't you put yourself into that category. Each of us is a creator, and it's essential to embrace that role, take control and shape our own reality with intent. I believe that sharing the thought processes that work for me may ignite something within you or even reaffirm your own ways of thinking. Use it as a base line, and make it your own. Anything and everything can be an opportunity for personal growth, should this be what you want for yourself – you have to not only want it, but you have to believe you deserve it and take the necessary steps in overcoming any mental barriers you may have in order to take action and make it your reality. I also don't believe in coincidences, so the very fact that you are holding this book is a sign that you are ready to take the next step in your own journey, so there we go – this is your sign and it is time for action. A close friend of mine, Sherene, loves looking for signs when she's about to make a life-altering decision and to some extent we all do, seeking that comfort of knowing we're on the right path. We all crave that reassurance, but here's the thing: even if you make a mistake, you can always learn and grow from it, adjust and keep going. So don't stress too much about aspects out of your control – rather focus on following your inner voice as to what feels right. You need to trust that inner knowing, that feeling that emerges once the fear has been stripped away. Ask yourself: if fear didn't exist here, what would I do? Does my decision align with the person I strive to be and the goals I'm aiming to achieve, in a dignified fashion? If you are not screaming "yes", then the answer is simply "no" – don't try to convince yourself that something or someone has the potential to be something it is not – potential is just not good enough in the present moment! Yet, even when the signs do appear, my friend would sometimes look for more signs, as if not fully trusting her intuition. I would then ask her: "How many more signs do you need to see before you trust the inner knowing and signs that reaffirm your decision?". We would generally share a giggle straight after, as my words ring true to her ears. I hope this is ringing true to your ears too. Trust the inner knowing – all the signs you need are already there.

Let's explore some of the thought processes and practicalities that drive me, as well as how we can tap into the universal intelligence available to us all - if we're willing to put in the effort. It's fascinating to consider how our mindset and actions can open up new pathways to understanding and connection. Without conscious intention, commitment, and a great deal of effort, particularly in the beginning, you are deluding yourself if you think spiritual awakening and growth will simply fall into your lap. It's a continuous, deliberate process that requires presence in every encounter, every experience. And how thrilling is that? There are undoubtedly multiple paths to achieve this, but if you're not quite there yet (and I believe we all have the potential to be), why not truly give yourself a chance? A genuine chance - not one of those half-hearted attempts that last a few days, weeks, or even months, only to fizzle out when it feels like too much effort. Then, before you know it, you slip back into old habits on autopilot, because it's what's familiar, what feels comfortable - even though it no longer serves you. Just take it a day at a time, without the pressure of doing it all over night, but surely one little bit at a time and watch the compound effects – no need to digest everything in one go and maybe even highlight the parts that speak to you, if that's something you like doing. Learning, reinventing yourself, growing as a person can really be fun, as it's supposed to be – what a gift to be able to do so, to expand your mind and your being one step at a time and realise your infinite capabilities. You should always weigh anything you read here, or anywhere else I suppose, with your own internal system and only take out what is beneficial to you, tweak it as necessary and make it your own. The reality though is that no great things happen in the comfort zone and sometimes just taking that leap out of the comfort zone is all it takes to change your life for the better. I took the leap many years ago when I decided to embrace what frightens me and pushes me out of my comfort zone. I'm not suggesting we do anything reckless here, but rather, I encourage stepping beyond the familiar into the unknown - the very place that often scares us. By shifting your perspective just a little bit and letting go of fear, allow yourself to step into the unknown with excitement. What lies beyond isn't something to dread – it's just you, an evolved and empowered version of you. The unknown is a gateway to growth, where change is the only constant. Embracing it means welcoming the opportunity to become more than you ever thought possible. Go after what you truly want, trusting that everything will align as it should. If things don't work out as you envisioned, don't just quit: keep moving forward and be open to adjusting your approach if you pick up on it being wrong for you – we only become rigid in our thinking when we're attached to a particular outcome. When we remain present, we remain flexible and adaptable. Hope and fear, though opposites in nature, are deeply interconnected and often keep us from living fully in the present moment. Hope projects us into an imagined future, building expectations that, when unmet, can lead to fear, disappointment, and frustration to mention a few. Fear, in turn, often stems from the gap between what we hoped for and the reality that actually unfolds. Together, they create a cycle that pulls us away from the present moment, leaving us restless and unfulfilled. Yet the present moment is where life truly exists and where authenticity, joy, and peace reside. By releasing attachment to both hopeful fantasies and fearful outcomes, we free ourselves to embrace what is, allowing life to unfold with greater clarity and contentment.

The answers you seek will come from within, so it's essential to learn how to tune into that inner guidance that you already possess, but that may be a little rusty. Trust your instincts, but make sure they're not influenced by fear or greed, because if they are, they'll guide you in the wrong direction. With time, you'll get the hang of it, and everything will start to make more sense as you practice tapping into your inner knowing. Even if you stumble in the beginning, and that's perfectly normal to do so, it's all part of the learning curve. Pay attention to that internal voice that guides you, even when you might not listen at first.

That's how you'll begin to discern what truly resonates with you and while you're on this journey, remember to stay grounded. If something seems too good to be true, it often is. There's a saying that reflects this well: "There's no such thing as a free lunch." It serves as a reminder to approach opportunities with a vigilant eye, recognising that what may appear effortless or without cost often comes with hidden strings or consequences, and sometimes that's fine too, but just be real with yourself about it. Staying aware helps us make more informed choices and avoid pitfalls that can arise from our own naivety. It's all about finding a balance between optimism and realism as we navigate our paths.

If you're anything like me, especially the much older versions of me, you might find it essential to recognise the many facets of who we are as we journey through life. I've often been my own worst critic, trapped in my own head where I would end up replaying various scenarios, analysing them senseless and that would naturally lead to feelings such as guilt, shame, anger or fear of recurrence. I would find myself revisiting past failures and punishing myself repeatedly for allowing them to unfold, for not knowing or doing better, and for not trusting my intuition. Yet, I've come to realise that these very lessons have taught me and guided me through life and have kept me moving forward. Each misstep is a stepping stone, helping me grow and navigate my journey with greater wisdom. I've learned the importance of being more graceful with myself and distinguishing between those past versions of me and who I am now, which will be different from who I am tomorrow, as I am continuously growing, learning and just be that extra bit more aligned with the ever changing and evolving version of myself. Acknowledging how far I've come allows me to be kinder with my self-talk, embracing my growth rather than fixating on my perceived shortcomings. This shift toward self-compassion has transformed my journey into one of acceptance and understanding, rather than harsh judgment.

You are capable of reaching anything you set your mind to and as such, it is important to find ways to expand your mind, to open up your heart and align the two, so that they can jointly guide you in any direction you choose. The trick is to stay true to yourself, to be your most authentic self (and for that you need to discover more about the essence of who you are), to stay connected/grounded, to stay humble and honest, to be more accepting of everything as it is and to just get out of your head per se for your mind is reluctant to take you to unfamiliar and scary places, yet ironically that's where you need to be to reach your fullest potential. What you want is on the other side of fear, where the unknown lives.

Part of my evolution has involved unlearning much of what I once thought I needed, while also discovering what truly resonates with me, aligning with my authentic self, and fully trusting my own judgment. I strive to exist in seamless synchronicity with every fibre of my being and letting go of worries about others' opinions, aspects outside my control, or the fear of disappointing people by saying "no" when saying "yes" would betray my own values. Nothing is worth compromising this inner harmony - not money, not fame, and certainly not the fleeting approval of others.

That said, I am keenly aware that we live in a material world, where bills need to be paid and practicalities demand attention. I, too, have found myself out of alignment at times - whether it's a loved one persuading me to do something I'd rather not or the allure of a seemingly "great" opportunity tempting me to stray. But I've come to realise that when we let go of fear, particularly the fear of where the money will come from, and instead trust in our ability to create, to act, and to believe in what we truly stand for, things tend to work out in one way or another. When we remove fear from the equation and act proactively, the resources we need often find their way to us. Trusting that our immediate needs will be met allows us to focus on alignment with our truth, rather than letting fear dictate our decisions. Staying true to yourself requires faith and persistence, but the payoff is a life that feels honest, meaningful, and truly your own.

The more I practice, the more aware I become, and the more I get it right. In this journey, I've also realised that kindness is a choice we can all make, a way we can respond to others, for you will agree everyone is fighting a battle we know nothing about and a little bit of kindness costs you absolutely nothing and goes such a long way. I know, you've heard this a million times over, but I am only repeating it, because I know the impact of kindness. Yet, at the same time it's essential not to neglect ourselves in the process either. We must continually ask: "Does this act of kindness align with me?". Balancing kindness towards others with self-compassion is crucial. You need to be kind to yourself first and foremost. When your cup is full, you'll have so much more to offer to others — let that overflow onto everyone that crosses your path, even strangers. Prioritising your own well-being allows you to show up fully and authentically in your relationships and pursuits. By nurturing yourself, you create a solid foundation from which you can extend kindness and support to those around you. Remember, self-compassion isn't selfish - it's absolutely essential for a balanced and fulfilling life. Embracing this truth not only enriches your own experience but also enhances your ability to uplift others along the way and it doesn't take much - prioritise "me time" when you're at your freshest and absolute best, perhaps first thing in the morning.

Wake up 15, 30 or 60 minutes earlier to accommodate this shift, whatever you can spare. Start small, but just start. Use that time to set the day up for success, whether through self-reflection, training, or preparing a healthy and nutritious meal. These small shifts can lead to significant changes in how you feel and how you engage with the world. Then just rinse and repeat – consistency is key.

Ultimately, our greatest gift on this earth is the ability to exercise free will, to direct and redirect our thoughts, refine our beliefs, align our actions and transform our lives as we choose, for our bodies merely take us to where our mind has already arrived. Take the time to position your mind as you desire – make sure your mind is there to serve you and not the other way around. Having that in mind, starting today, you call the shots as to who you want to be, where you want to be, who you want to be associated with and how you want to live. Set clear intentions and write them down, because just like in science where every action has a reaction, your choices have consequences, and writing them down becomes something tangible and no longer just a fragment of your imagination that merely passed through, along with countless more thoughts. After thoughtful reflection, you might need to let go of certain aspects of your current self and lifestyle to make room for the new version of you, so don't go and hold on too tight to who you are today and allow yourself to become that much more. This mirrors the yin-yang concept, give and take, cause and effect, and various others which ultimately lead to the same base principles around balance, reciprocity and interconnectedness, when it comes to the functioning of the universe and human existence.

Having said all of that – do not take my word or that of anybody else for granted, but process through your own internal channels and see what rings true and to what extent. Let that stick. Let that grow and translate into all areas of your life.

You'll know you're on the right path when you start to feel an inner calm and a sense of joy that arises for no particular reason at all. You do not need a reason to feel this way – this can literally be your state of being. This joy doesn't depend on external circumstances, on someone else validating it, it's a deep-seated sense of contentment that emerges when you embrace gratitude in its fullest form whilst embracing the present moment as it is. It's important to realise that you don't need a specific reason to feel joyful or at peace. This feeling isn't about the absence of challenges or imperfections, but rather, it stems from an acceptance of everything as it is in this very moment and a sense of knowing that you can handle anything that comes your way, at the appropriate time and in the appropriate way.

This shift in perspective is subtle yet profound. When you begin to recognise that peace and joy exist within you - not as fleeting emotions, but as a state of being, you free yourself from the endless search for external validation. You stop looking to circumstances, people, or achievements to determine your happiness and instead, cultivate a deep-rooted appreciation for life as it unfolds.

When you cultivate this sense of gratitude, you begin to appreciate life for what it is and not just the highlights, but the entire tapestry, irrespective of what that may look like. This kind of joy comes from shifting your focus away from what's missing or what's "flawed" in your life. Instead of getting caught up in a cycle of wanting or comparing, you learn to celebrate the present, finding beauty and value in your experiences, no matter how small or mundane they may seem. Gratitude, in this sense, isn't merely about recognising the good things, but it's about embracing all aspects of your life, including the struggles and imperfections. Those challenges often come bearing the gifts of hidden lessons and wisdom you may not have necessarily learnt under different circumstances. When you face difficulties with an open heart, you can uncover insights that contribute to your growth and understanding. Each experience, whether joyful or painful, adds depth to your journey and enriches your perspective.

Acceptance is key to this process. When you welcome your circumstances with an open heart, gratitude naturally follows. You start to see the lessons and value in every experience, even the tough ones or should I say, especially the tough ones. This mindset transforms challenges into opportunities for growth, making every moment, no matter how ordinary or difficult, feel meaningful. Through this lens, joy becomes a byproduct of a deep-seated appreciation for life itself. You begin to understand that life is a mix of light and dark, and both are essential to the human experience. By welcoming everything with gratitude, you create a foundation for lasting joy that transcends fleeting moments and connects you to a more profound sense of fulfillment.

Just remember, acceptance isn't passive-it's the first active step towards self-improvement.

2 EVERYTHING IS ENERGY

In the grand tapestry of existence, the idea that everything is energy serves as a profound and unifying principle. Everything in the universe, from atoms to the air we breathe, is composed of energy, manifesting in various forms like light, heat, and kinetic energy. All matter, thoughts, emotions, and interactions vibrate at different frequencies, with each entity possessing its own unique vibrational print if you like. This interconnectedness highlights that our thoughts and emotions not only shape our own experiences but also influence those around us, creating a ripple effect in our surroundings. The common thread connecting past, present, and future generations is the shared human experience, which at its core is energy. This energy transcends time, cycling through generations, influencing and being influenced by those before and after us. Just as our ancestors' energy created the world we inhabit today, our own energy flows outward, shaping the present and building the foundation for future generations. In this way, we are all interconnected, part of a continuous energetic legacy that binds humanity together across time. Fancy, right?

Understanding that everything is energy fundamentally shapes how I approach relationships and interactions. Every thought, feeling, word and action carries energy, and the way we exchange it with others determines the quality of our connections, experiences and to a large extent, quality of life. With this in mind, tough love in the form of personal boundaries becomes not just a method of interaction but an energetic practice - one that protects my energy while encouraging others to cultivate their own.

When I set boundaries or hold someone accountable, I am not withdrawing love or compassion. On the contrary, I am redirecting the energy of our relationship toward growth and balance. Allowing someone to continually take from my energy without reciprocity or accountability not only depletes me but also enables their stagnation or self-destructive behaviour. Tough love is about breaking that cycle, ensuring that the energy we share remains constructive and mutually respectful. Here, it's about saying the right things at the right time, with kindness, and you'll know best what that looks like – it need not be harsh, argumentative or in a fashion that feeds the ego.

For those I care about, practicing tough love means recognising their capacity to grow and thrive, even when it requires difficult conversations or actions. Love, at its deepest level, isn't about shielding others from the consequences of their choices: it's about empowering them to face life with honesty and strength and I am all about enabling others to do this for themselves, should this be what they want of course. By challenging someone to take responsibility, I'm not just protecting myself, but I am also offering them the opportunity to realign their own energy, to move from a place of struggle or harm to one of accountability and empowerment.

This practice also nurtures authenticity in my relationships. When I act with honesty and firmness, I send a message that our bond is strong enough to withstand discomfort, that I value the connection enough to prioritise its health. Tough love creates an energetic space where both parties can grow - where compassion meets truth, vulnerability meets accountability, and support meets self-respect. The relationships that don't stick were clearly not meant to, so don't sweat over it too much and be grateful for the lessons and experiences that came from it. Where you've been the one in the wrong, acknowledge it and perhaps express it to the other, for it is important to do so as part of the accountability journey.

Ultimately, tough love aligns with the principle that energy must flow freely and constructively to sustain balance and harmony. It acknowledges that I have a responsibility to myself and my loved ones to maintain this flow by being kind yet firm, empathetic yet resolute. By setting boundaries and practicing accountability, I not only safeguard my energy but also encourage others to strengthen and redirect their own. This mutual respect of energy fosters relationships that are not only healthy and sustainable but deeply transformative, honouring the interconnectedness of all beings.

Not everyone will appreciate or be deserving of the energy you invest in them, and that's an important truth to accept. Some may resist accountability or see your boundaries as a threat to their comfort. However, the key is that you've acted from a place of integrity, and in doing so, you've done right by them. Those who are misaligned with your values or your energetic intentions will gradually fall away, as relationships, just like everything else, naturally shift toward alignment. This process can be difficult, but it's also liberating. Energetic takers i.e. those who drain rather than contribute to the balance of a relationship - often won't value your boundaries or your tough love. They thrive on manipulation or need constant reassurance, demanding energy without offering reciprocity. Over time, these relationships will fade as you reinforce your boundaries and protect your energy. By practicing tough love and standing firm in your convictions, you create the space for healthier, more balanced connections to flourish. You may lose some, but what remains will be authentic and energising, rooted in mutual respect and shared growth.

It's essential to approach these situations and individuals with gratitude, despite the challenges they may present. Energetic takers, those who resist growth or continually drain your energy, serve a deeper purpose. They bring awareness to your boundaries, illuminating where you need to stand firm and where growth is required. These experiences push you to redefine your sense of self and your standards for relationships, opening doors to a whole new version of you. In navigating these dynamics, you learn more about your worth, your limits, and what you truly need in order to thrive. They teach you the importance of self-respect, of not compromising your energy for the sake of others' comfort or approval. Over time, you evolve into a person who knows exactly what you will and will not accept, someone who cultivates relationships built on mutual respect and alignment. In this way, the struggles with misaligned people actually set the stage for more meaningful, energising interactions. They shape a new way of being, one where you move through the world with clarity, purpose, and an unwavering commitment to your highest self, which is your authentic self.

How often do we pick up on the emotions of others - whether it's sharing a laugh, connecting through a moment of sadness, or even feeling the intensity of an angry outburst? Our ability to attune ourselves to the emotional energy around us is a powerful skill, but it can also blur the lines between what is ours and what belongs to others. This is why it's essential to develop the ability to distinguish between the two, allowing us to navigate our emotional landscape with clarity and intention. The key to this lies in cultivating a deep awareness of our own feelings, which I practice through regular check-ins with myself. By doing so, I can identify when I'm absorbing the emotions of others, whether they're experiencing joy, sadness, or frustration, and separate those from my own emotional state.

At the same time, it's important to recognise that others are also battling their own perceived inadequacies and struggles. As we navigate our own emotional terrain, we must remain compassionate and kind, understanding that everyone is facing their own challenges. Yet, as we extend empathy, we must also honour our own emotional boundaries and not take on the weight of others' burdens. Emotional struggles, whether our own or someone else's, can easily intertwine, and this is where self-awareness becomes a tool for resilience.

By distinguishing between the emotions that belong to us and those that come from others, we can engage with the world more authentically and protect our energy. This practice of self-awareness and emotional clarity creates space for kindness without compromise, compassion without enabling, and growth without overextending ourselves. In navigating both our own emotions and the emotional landscape of others, we empower ourselves to engage in relationships and situations from a place of strength, understanding, and intentionality.

This reflection helps me understand my triggers and patterns, giving me insight into why I might feel or react a certain way. Incorporating mindfulness into my daily life has also transformed how I approach my emotions. By observing my feelings without judgment, I can acknowledge them as they arise, irrespective of whether it's joy, sadness, anger, or confusion - without allowing those emotions to take over and overwhelm me. This non-attachment allows me to respond more thoughtfully rather than react impulsively. I've learned the importance of distinguishing my emotions from those of others as it does happen that now and then I absorb the energy around me and the moment I feel a shift in my own energy, I pause and ask myself if these feelings are genuinely mine or if I'm picking up on someone else's emotional state. This kind of awareness empowers me to set boundaries and protect my emotional well-being and release it swiftly.

As I've navigated my own journey, I've come to understand how deeply personal introspection and growth shape what we achieve in our lifetimes. My experiences have shown me that our energy not only attracts specific circumstances but also influences how we engage with the world. For instance, when I cultivate self-awareness and embrace my emotions - whatever they may be, I notice a shift in how I interact with others and how they respond to me. This dynamic interplay between my inner states and external realities underscores the idea that I have the power to shape my path through intention and awareness. Just as magnets with the same polarity repel each other, while opposite poles are drawn together by an unseen force, the energy we carry within us attracts experiences, people, and circumstances that resonate with it. When you radiate gratitude, contentment, and peace, you naturally draw more of the same into your life. Conversely, when your focus is on lack, resentment, or fear, you may find yourself repeatedly encountering situations that reinforce those very emotions.

This isn't about blind positivity or pretending struggles don't exist, but rather it's about recognizing that the energy you put out into the world shapes what returns to you. Just as magnets with opposite poles are drawn together by an unseen force, we are constantly exchanging energy with our surroundings, attracting experiences that reflect our internal state. When you cultivate a mindset of openness and appreciation, you align yourself with opportunities, relationships, and moments that resonate at the same frequency.

Recognising the full spectrum of feelings, whether happiness, anger, sadness, or fear has been essential for me as each emotion carries its own message and purpose. Instead of labelling feelings as "good" or "bad", I've come to see them as natural responses to my experiences, again, shifting my internal definitions or belief systems. Emotions like anger or sadness can offer valuable insights into my needs and desires or even safety, depending on the circumstances. This shift in perception allows me to learn from my feelings and use them as guides for personal growth. At times, navigating your own emotional landscape can feel overwhelming, and seeking support from someone who can offer a fresh perspective can be incredibly helpful. However, in most circumstances, simply sitting with myself, something I often choose to do, allows me to arrive at the clarity I need. I trust myself fully and rely on my inner knowing. That said, sharing emotions can be valuable in processing them, and sometimes, an outside perspective is all it takes. My husband and I often do this for each other, offering insights that help us see things more clearly.

When emotions become too intense, I turn to grounding techniques such as deep breathing, meditation, writing, pilates, or spending time in nature. These practices help me reconnect with the present moment and cultivate a sense of calm. While it's not always possible to regulate emotions instantly, I've learned that we have the ability to talk ourselves through almost anything. Setting clear intentions for how I want to feel or respond in specific situations has been instrumental in guiding my emotional navigation. By consciously choosing how to engage with my emotions, I align my energy with my desired outcomes.

Embracing the fluidity of emotions is also essential. Just as the seasons change, so do our emotional states. This understanding allows me to move through difficult moments with greater ease, knowing that no feeling is permanent - both challenges and happy moments will come and go. As a woman, I've also become deeply aware of how our hormonal cycle influences this emotional ebb and flow. Each month, we experience shifts that affect our mood, energy, and perspective. And while this may primarily resonate with women, men should take note too - understanding these natural cycles fosters empathy and support, ultimately strengthening relationships. The menstrual cycle mirrors the seasons, each phase bringing its own challenges and opportunities:

Menstrual Phase (Winter) – This phase marks the beginning of the cycle, often characterised by lower energy and a natural pull toward rest and reflection. It's a time to embrace stillness, honour your body's need for care, and practice self-compassion. Gentle activities like journaling, light stretching, or simply slowing down can be profoundly restorative.

Follicular Phase (Spring) – As estrogen rises, energy, creativity, and optimism return. This is a period of renewal, perfect for setting intentions, planning projects, and embracing new challenges. Think of it as a fresh start, which is ideal for brainstorming, trying new things, and stepping into your power.

Ovulatory Phase (Summer) – This is the peak of the cycle, marked by high energy, confidence, and natural magnetism. Social interactions, communication, and collaborations feel effortless. It's a powerful time to connect with others, express ideas, and take decisive action.

Luteal Phase (Autumn) – As progesterone rises and estrogen dips, emotions may intensify, and a need for solitude or introspection emerges. Many women, myself included, find this phase challenging due to increased sensitivity and irritability. Recognising these shifts and responding with extra self-compassion is key. Practices like mindfulness, journaling, and gentle movement can help manage heightened emotions. This is also a good time to complete tasks, reflect on priorities, and prepare for the cycle to begin anew.

By understanding these phases and how they influence emotions and energy, we can approach each one with greater awareness and care. For women, this knowledge fosters self-compassion, while for men, it offers clarity and an opportunity to provide support and empathy to the women in their lives. Embracing the rhythm of these cycles leads to deeper connections, with ourselves and with others, and a greater appreciation for the innate wisdom of the body.

Embracing this understanding encourages personal responsibility. It invites me to reflect on how my thoughts and emotions shape my reality. Instead of feeling like a victim of circumstance, I recognise that I hold the agency to influence how I feel, which in turn influences my quality of life. This empowerment has been transformative: through practices like mindfulness and creative expression, I've been able to shift my energy, opening myself up to new possibilities and personal growth.

Moreover, this perspective fosters a holistic view of life,

where the physical, emotional, and spiritual dimensions are interconnected. As I've recognised the energetic nature of everything, I've begun to see myself as part of a larger whole, intertwined with all beings and the universe at large. This awareness has cultivated empathy and compassion, deepening my understanding of our shared humanity. At the core, all human beings want to feel a sense of meaning, connection, and fulfilment. We seek love and belonging, the assurance that we matter, and the freedom to express our true selves and for us to just be accepted as we are. Whether through relationships, achievements, or personal growth, our deepest desire is often to experience joy, peace, and a life that feels purposeful. Beneath all the surface differences such as our different cultures, body shapes and sizes, religions, ambitions, or circumstances - this shared longing for connection, understanding, and a life well-lived unites us all. We need to focus a little more on what connects us versus what divides us.

Each interaction carries its own energetic exchange, influencing how we connect with one another. I've learned that my emotional state can resonate with others, creating harmonious connections or leading to misunderstandings. By being mindful of my own energy and intentions, I strive to nurture healthier, more supportive relationships that enrich my life and those of others.

As I navigate this energetic landscape, the role of intention becomes increasingly clear. My intentions act as a guiding force, directing my energy toward specific outcomes. When I set clear intentions, I find that my energy aligns more closely with my desires, facilitating the manifestation of opportunities that resonate with my true self. This alignment enhances my ability to navigate challenges and pursue my goals with clarity and purpose.

At last, embracing the idea that everything is energy has transformed my understanding of reality. It has invited me to explore the depths of my consciousness and engage with the world around me in a more intentional and meaningful way. Recognizing the energy within and around me empowers me to create the life I desire, fostering growth, connection, and a deeper appreciation for the beauty of existence.

In this energetic journey, I've learned that my inner world profoundly shapes my outer experiences. By cultivating awareness of my thoughts, feelings, and intentions, I open myself to the limitless possibilities that life offers. This process allows me to recognize how my mindset influences my interactions and the opportunities I attract. When I focus on my intentions and embrace my emotions, I create a resonant energy that draws similar vibrations into my life. The dance of energy continues, inviting me to participate, evolve, and embrace the profound interconnectedness of all things. As I navigate this flow, I find a deeper sense of belonging, purpose, and harmony within the vibrant universe we share. Each moment becomes an invitation to explore, to learn, and to connect more deeply with myself and those around me. This ongoing journey enhances my appreciation for life's richness, revealing that every experience, whether joyful or challenging, serves as a teacher. By remaining open and receptive, I cultivate resilience and adaptability, allowing me to move through life with grace. This interplay between my inner landscape and the outer world fosters a holistic sense of well-being, grounding me in the knowledge that I am an integral part of something much larger, and in that realization, I find both strength and serenity.

Ultimately, to be human means embracing the fluidity of life, which I believe applies to us all - the constant change, the challenges, and the countless opportunities to evolve. It means understanding that we are all part of a larger, interconnected web of energy, where our actions, emotions, and growth impact not only ourselves but those we share this journey with. In this way, being human is both a beautiful and humbling experience, one that requires us to continuously seek our own truth whilst remaining objective, which is where we find our balance, authenticity, and compassion as we navigate the ebb and flow of life.

Our strengths are our vulnerabilities, and this paradox is one of the most profound truths of the human experience and one of my personal biggest lessons. Strength does not come from being invulnerable or perfect, but from embracing the very aspects of ourselves that make us human such as our emotions, our capacity for connection, our attunement to the world around us. It's in our vulnerabilities that we find the greatest strength and potential for growth, because they are often the gateways to deeper understanding and connection. When we allow ourselves to be vulnerable, we open the door to authenticity, where true strength resides.

Know who you can open up to and who you shouldn't, or at least not in this very moment. Your time, energy, and vulnerability are valuable, and not everyone is deserving of them. People vibrate at different frequencies, influenced by their state of being - their mindset, emotions, and intentions. Higher frequencies are often associated with positivity, love, and authenticity, while lower frequencies can reflect negativity, fear, or dishonesty. While we all have the capacity to vibrate at higher frequencies, not everyone chooses to or is ready to do so on a more regular basis. Paying attention to these differences helps you discern who is safe to trust and who might misuse your openness. For example, the ability to feel deeply - whether it's love, grief, or joy, is both a vulnerability and a strength. It makes us susceptible to pain, but it also opens us to the most profound experiences of life. Our vulnerability allows us to connect with others on a deeply human level, to empathize, and to share in their joy and sorrow. However, this emotional openness should be shared selectively, with those who align with our energy and can both honour the depth of our feelings as well as respect our boundaries.

The strength of vulnerability lies in the courage to be seen fully, without hiding behind walls or armour. When we embrace this and share ourselves with the right people, we foster compassion, intimacy, and meaningful relationships. At the same time, we must protect our energy and be mindful of those who might not respect our openness, especially in a professional setting. By creating safe spaces for growth and mutual understanding, we invite others to do the same, cultivating connections that enrich our lives.

Furthermore, our vulnerabilities help us to navigate challenges with resilience. It's when we acknowledge and lean into our fears, insecurities, and imperfections that we find the resources within us to transform them into strengths. Facing our vulnerabilities head-on allows us to build emotional intelligence and mental fortitude, teaching us how to adapt to change and remain grounded in the midst of adversity. In this way, our vulnerabilities are not weaknesses to be ashamed of but invitations to evolve and expand into the fullest version of ourselves.

In embracing the interconnectedness of all things and recognizing our vulnerabilities as strengths, we create a life that is not only authentic but also deeply aligned with our purpose and values. The flow of life, its challenges and transformations becomes a dance of growth, where every vulnerability is an opportunity to build deeper resilience, greater wisdom, and stronger connections with others.

Where you place your attention is where you direct your energy. What you focus on expands, shaping your beliefs, influencing your words, and guiding your actions. Over time, these become your habits, define your character, and ultimately shape your destiny. Be mindful of what you entertain: some things are worth nurturing, while others are best released. Remember, where attention goes, energy flows, so choose wisely, not only shaping your future but also defining your present.

3 PEELING BACK THE LAYERS

Where we come from, the way we have experienced life to date, through our personal observations and surroundings certainly shapes our perceptions of what life should be like and influences our multilayered identities to some extent, but it doesn't have to define us or limit us in any such way. Our backgrounds provide context for the experiences that we have had and what we have endured, affecting our values, beliefs, and perspectives. The core struggles we face as human beings often revolve around identity and self-discovery, emotional and mental well-being, connection and relationships, control and uncertainty, purpose and fulfillment, mortality and acceptance of impermanence, as well as balance and boundaries. These struggles are not limited to internal battles but are often shaped by external forces, such as socio-economic challenges and societal obstacles, which can create feelings of limitation, exclusion, or injustice. Yet, it is through navigating these experiences, whether they stem from financial hardship, personal loss, emotional turmoil, or the pressure to meet societal expectations, that we cultivate resilience, deepen our empathy, and discover inner strength. In embracing both the personal and collective challenges we face, we not only move closer to our authentic selves but also contribute to a more compassionate and connected world. These same struggles are the ones that keep resurfacing in all of our lives, in one or other form. Despite everything we have been through to date, we can all agree that we are our own individuals, emerging through our birth parents, regardless of their level of involvement or lack thereof and irrespective of the type of impact they may have had on us. We are however not our parents, and while we may have assumed some of their struggles, often without even realising it, especially if they haven't dealt with those themselves, it's crucial to recognise and differentiate those challenges from our own. This process often involves acknowledging our inner child, the part of us that carries the emotions and experiences of our early years, some of which may have been deeply suppressed as a copying mechanism, but by peeling back the various layers and nurturing this inner child, we can understand how past wounds and traumas may influence our present behaviour and circumstances, allowing us to offer compassion without taking on the burdens that aren't ours to carry. Perhaps one of the big lessons we are meant to learn is how to be true to the very essence that is us or figuratively speaking "release" those parts of us which were never ours to begin with, while forging our own paths. Our identities are multifaceted, influenced not only by our pasts in the family home, but also by external relationships, education, interests, and personal journeys and so much more. Recognising that we are not defined by our backgrounds can be empowering, encouraging self-reflection and growth as we pursue our goals and visions. Ultimately, our backgrounds serve as a foundation from which we can build, allowing us to boldly pursue who we want to become or rather, who we've always been, free from the constraints of our past. This may involve expansion on existing foundations, or rebuilding from scratch, which sometimes makes more sense instead of trying to build on rotten foundations, which inevitably can only crumble down as the structures may not be strong enough to carry the weight. You can sit with yourself and see what you need to do to get to where you want to be as this is very much an individual journey and you need not compare such to anyone else's as that's just irrelevant and counterproductive. It's important however in this process to embrace all parts of yourself and to speak to your inner child with the utmost love, kindness and understanding for that inner child has done its very best with whatever was presented to it, in order to persevere and deal with feelings which were likely too big to handle, without having the capability or skills necessary to deal with.

As I sit with myself, I unravel all sorts of bottled-up emotions, deeply suppressed and put away in a place where even I had to scratch around to find them. Of course, this is a very common way of "dealing" with feelings we don't understand or know how to process and release. These emotions, if left unresolved can make us feel lost, uncomfortable, incapable, unworthy, or just plain heavy, with the constant replay of certain scenarios. For much of my life, I wasn't allowed to sit with my difficult emotions or otherwise express them, because they made those around me feel uneasy and I had to remain strong, not just for me, but for those around me too. It's a vicious little cycle that keeps repeating itself and most of us end up going through life without truly understanding ourselves and if we are unable to understand ourselves, we could never truly understand others and what an injustice to the world that would be, mainly to our own world. Lacking the guidance or tools to release emotions in a healthy way, I had to carve my own path using whatever resources were available to me at the time. In doing so, my brain stepped in as my protector, activating its default settings at a young age. It did what it needed to keep me going, often shielding me from harm, but at a cost, as it distorted my perceptions of certain realities, relationships, and even convinced me of false truths in its effort to protect me. Over time, this defence mechanism blurred my vision, dulled my intuition, and eroded my trust in my own judgment. I began to doubt myself, knowing there was a 50% chance my instincts might be wrong – a bit of a gamble. This is the nature of the brain when left unchecked - it operates in default mode, which isn't usually aligned with our higher self – it's rather primitive and unrefined at its core. To me, the brain is a powerful tool now, but it shouldn't be the sole operator of our internal system. When allowed to run the show, it suppresses emotions by adding a story to each one of them, instead of releasing them, as that's all valuable information for preventing distress, harm or otherwise undesired outcomes which it naturally wants to keep full record of. It meticulously files unresolved feelings with its corresponding story into the subconscious mind - what I've come to think of as a wastebasket for everything we avoid, fear to confront or just don't know how to confront. To reclaim control, we must activate and integrate the wisdom of our higher self, using the brain as a tool rather than letting it define our reality. Like any wastebasket left unattended, there's an inevitable spillover and what spills out is rarely pleasant. Guilt, shame, embarrassment, anger, or confusion emerge seemingly out of nowhere, leaving us wondering why we feel so triggered in certain scenarios and what in the world is wrong with us. The truth is, every time a present situation echoes an unresolved past emotion which is attached to a story we tell ourselves, the subconscious wastebasket tips over, forcing us to relive those suppressed feelings, which is really just another opportunity to deal with them and only now do I realise this. This endless loop can be painful, exhausting, and is just so unnecessary - a form of self-inflicted suffering, unless we decide to exit the loop and deal with it and we can. I've realised it's time to clear out this accumulated emotional "waste" and in calling it waste I do not wish to invalidate it in any way, but rather, I'm acknowledging that the accumulated effects have weighed me down and have turned into something burdensome. I no longer want to live with the weight of bottled-up emotions that spill over into my present life. I no longer need the safety mechanisms my brain created ages ago to shield me from harm or the tendency to anticipate the worst case scenario as a means of self-protection. Living in fear and suffering can rob a person from experiencing joy and disconnecting them from the abundant blessings in life. This is why we need to see things for what they truly are and stop bottling up and holding on to what is meant to be released and even worse, imagining worst case scenarios that do not even exist. Suppressing our emotions only creates cycles of pain, suffering, and repetition. Instead, we should embrace the courage to be truth-seekers and to see the world as it is – not any better or any worse, but just as it is. We need to be mindful of the risk of misalignment that comes from what we think, what we believe, what we communicate and what we do. You can perceive yourself to be a certain way, possibly a kind, spiritual person but if your thoughts, speech and actions are misaligned and aren't genuinely authentic, you'll experience turbulence that will be felt not only within you but all the way around you, in your relationship with yourself and others. We can only move forwards and upwards when we're in synchronicity with ourselves, our thoughts, our beliefs and actions. For that, we have to be honest with ourselves and see things exactly as they are – not in any way distorted through a lens of fear or greed. How do we align with ourself, for the highest good? Stay true to yourself, to who you are and who you want to be, don't lie and make sure your actions match it all. Say what you mean and mean what you say-don't waste time on manipulative or "strategic" games for that will leave you misaligned. This doesn't mean to go and be inconsiderate or hurtful to others in terms of your delivery but rather the contrary - always ensure the timing for the truth is appropriate and delivered in a considerate manner in terms of the recipient, and depending on the context and particular circumstances, doing so in private may be the considerate thing to do. Also, don't go out of your way to tell people what you think they could do better without them having asked you, especially if it's in relation to something that they are likely to be sensitive about. You should also know the difference between someone genuinely wanting to improve and know the truth, versus someone seeking validation and their lack of ability to handle the truth. Be gentle on those people for they haven't reached a state of evolution necessary to embrace the full truth.

If they want your opinion, they'll ask, as that generally can be interpreted as a cue that they're ready to receive it. Always be kind in your delivery of the truth, whatever that may look like. It's a lot easier to deliver the truth when it's of a positive nature and little to no guidance is necessary there, but when the delivery is of something a little more sensitive in nature, focus on the positives first and when the time is right address any constructive criticism in a considerate manner. People are sensitive and people are generally struggling and often very unaware.

When we align our thoughts, words, and actions with honesty and authenticity, we strengthen our ability to trust our own judgment and we can move through life with a sense of calm. In doing so, we can make decisions with confidence, knowing they are grounded in clarity and truth rather than fear or confusion. By addressing our emotions head-on and clearing the wastebasket of our subconscious, one little bit at a time, we free ourselves from the shackles of the past. We allow space for growth, joy, and inner peace. We become empowered to face life's challenges with unwavering strength, secure in the knowledge that our intuition is clear and our judgment is sound. All of this then translates into all areas of our lives and that is so powerful. When experiencing any emotion, it triggers a chemical reaction in the body that sends a signal to the brain which lasts approximately 90 seconds in terms of Dr Jill Taylor's neuroscientific observation and during this time the brain releases neurotransmitters and hormones that create the physical sensations associated with that emotion, whatever it may be, such as a racing heart, tightness in the chest, shallow breathing sweating, chills or tears. After those 90 seconds have lapsed, if we continue to feel that very emotion, it is because our mind is choosing to keep replaying the thought or story we tell ourselves that triggered the emotion in the first place. This insight is powerful because it shows us that we are not victims of our emotions and that we have the ability to observe, process, and let them pass through us if we choose not to feed the emotional loop with repetitive thoughts. Time it next time it happens to you and after the 90 seconds are up, make a conscious decision as to what follows – you can continue to feed the emotion and end up in the loop situation or you can intercept it. Life is full of choices and we get to choose what happens next.

Clearing the wastebasket of the subconscious begins with the courageous act of facing the experiences that created those unresolved feelings. It requires us to revisit the moments that shaped our pain, fear, or doubt and to give them the acknowledgment they deserve. By facing these experiences, we validate our emotions instead of suppressing them. We accept that it was okay to feel the way we did at the time, that our reactions were a natural response to our circumstances, even if they were imperfect or messy. Once acknowledged, the next step is to "release" these emotions. This involves recognising that they no longer serve us. The coping mechanisms we developed were necessary then, but we are no longer the same person we were back then. We've grown, we've learnt a thing or two. We are now capable of handling similar challenges with calm, patience, and wisdom, rather than reacting impulsively like an overwhelmed child and my reference here is very much intentional – a child's brain is still developing, particularly the prefrontal cortex, which governs logic, decision-making, impulse control, and self-regulation. These functions do not fully mature until the mid-twenties, although emotional maturity is not guaranteed with age nor a given - it requires conscious effort, self-awareness, and intentional growth. As the prefrontal cortex develops, it gradually integrates with other brain areas, such as the amygdala, which processes emotions, and this development helps us regulate our reactions more effectively as adults. Factors such as childhood trauma, emotional neglect, chronic stress, and societal conditioning can disrupt this process and make it harder for the brain to effectively regulate emotions and respond with wisdom. As a result, some adults remain stuck in reactive patterns, driven by fear, impulse, and emotional triggers, much like a child whose brain is still developing. This happens because the prefrontal cortex is not fully integrated with the amygdala. However, the brain's neuroplasticity allows us to rewire these patterns at any stage of life. Through self-awareness, mindfulness, and emotional healing, we can strengthen this connection and shift from reacting impulsively to responding with calm, patience, and wisdom. In doing so, we break free from unconscious patterns rooted in our past and begin to live more consciously and authentically.

Releasing these accumulated emotions isn't about forgetting or denying the past - it's about letting go of the hold it has on us. It's about choosing not to carry its weight forward. To clear the wastebasket, we must also remind ourselves that past experiences do not define who we are – they are just that: experiences. They are chapters in our story, but they are not the entirety of it. We can rewrite the narrative of our lives by choosing how we respond now. Dwelling on past pain only robs us of the beauty and potential of the present moment. Instead of allowing those moments to dictate our actions, we can use them as stepping stones to build a stronger, more self-aware foundation. We deserve inner peace. We deserve to know ourselves deeply - not as the sum of our wounds, but as resilient, evolving and joyful beings. By facing and releasing the baggage of the past, we create space to live with clarity and intention. This process helps us move through life with purpose, aligning our actions with our true values and desires. When we free ourselves from the patterns of pain and suppression, we step into the present moment fully.

We regain the ability to embrace life with an open heart, to experience joy without reservation, and to approach challenges with grace. We honour our journey not by being anchored to past pain or overly attached to fleeting joys but by embracing the flow of life as it unfolds. Both clinging to wounds and holding tightly to positive emotions can trap us in expectations that life, in its ever-changing nature, may not meet. Perhaps some pursuits are not about capturing and retaining, but experiencing, savouring, or aligning with. Like standing still to feel the sun on your face, sometimes fulfilment comes when we stop chasing and start being. Heraclitus reminds us that life is constant transformation, just like a river that changes with every moment, so do we. True strength lies in appreciating our growth, trusting our resilience, and facing the future with an open heart and a steady mind, ready for whatever flows our way and remembering the words of Heraclitus that: "No man ever steps in the same river twice, for it's not the same river and he's not the same man". Another great consideration to have is that only dead fish go with the flow, which is the original version of this saying, however, I would like to add, unless it's the flow of life per se or in other words, only dead fish are carried by the current and awake souls get to become one with the current.

Our thought patterns and belief systems are deeply interconnected, and understanding their impact can profoundly enhance our emotional well-being and in turn, quality of life. To explore this, it's important to reflect on the very important question: "Who am I and what makes me, 'me'?". While the physical elements, actions, and experiences play roles in shaping our identity or rather the way we perceive our identity to be, they do not define who we are. To find that out, you have to take a deep dive inwards. Research in psychology and philosophy suggests that our sense of self transcends the aforementioned elements, indicating that we are part of something far greater and more profound, than we can fully comprehend.

The physical element, whilst influential at first glance, is not the determinant of who we are at our core. Many people may find it challenging to look beyond the obvious, but it's important to remember that this journey of self-discovery often brings us closer to breaking through those barriers, little bit at a time. Each step taken is a move toward embracing a fuller, richer understanding of ourselves. Studies in self-perception highlight that our self-worth and identity are shaped by a multitude of factors beyond just physical attributes. Similarly, our actions and experiences contribute to our sense of self, but they are parts of a larger narrative. For instance, research in existential psychology suggests that our actions and experiences are important, yet they form just one aspect of our broader existence. It is thus imperative when seeking the answers around self to look at the broader picture, for looking into any particular aspect in isolation, just like in law or anything else, will provide you with a disconnected answer.

The idea that we are more than our physical, behavioural, and experiential components is supported by the notion of a larger interconnected system. Biophysics and systems theory propose that we are part of an intricate web of energy and interactions, contributing to and influenced by a greater whole, which is available to all. This perspective aligns with the idea that we are embedded in a vast, dynamic field of existence that extends beyond our individual selves, and ultimately one that we all have access to – a unified field of consciousness, from which matter emerges.

Here I'd like to mention the Hundredth Monkey Phenomenon, which refers to a phenomenon observed in the 1950's involving Japanese macaques. Researchers, including Dr Keith Chen and Dr Lyall Watson, studied a group of macaques on Koshima Island, where they noted that some monkeys began washing sweet potatoes before eating them. Initially, only a few monkeys practiced this behaviour, but once the number of individuals reached a critical mass, often cited as around one hundred, there was a sudden increase in the behaviour among both those monkeys and others on nearby islands who had never been exposed to this method. Although this study is deeply critiqued within the scientific community for its lack of rigorous data and the challenges of replicating its findings, it continues to spark conversations about the possibility of collective consciousness and social learning. The idea suggests that once a certain threshold of awareness is reached, new behaviours or insights might ripple through a population, inspiring reflections on how knowledge and cultural practices can transcend individual experiences. My own opinion on the matter is that in order for you to have access into the infinite pool of information you would have to align your vibrations or in more practical terms your way of living, thinking and being and consciousness with the unified field that connects all beings. Tuning into your inner wisdom serves as a powerful form of energetic guidance, so listen closely to your inner knowing and the subtle nudges from your mind and body, alongside the setting of your clear intention to do so, followed by the act of surrendering to the flow of energy and trusting that you are part of a greater whole which will allow the insights you need to come to you when you are ready to receive them.

Our subjective experiences such as how we interpret and engage with the world reflect this broader connection, and I believe the ability to still the mind, allows us to move past this point, because the unifying principle is consciousness.

According to constructivist theories in psychology, our perceptions and interpretations shape our realities, suggesting that we are creators of our own experiences, and I couldn't agree more. This aligns with the notion that our true essence is part of a larger, more complex system, one that encompasses more than just our immediate perceived realities.

Consider the remarkable capabilities of our bodies and minds, which demonstrate an intelligence and interconnectedness that extend beyond mere physical processes. The concept of homeostasis, the body's ability to maintain internal stability, exemplifies this intricate balance. Similarly, the field of neuroplasticity reveals that our brains are capable of significant adaptation and growth, reflecting our potential to evolve beyond our current state if we are brave and consistent enough to transcend the limits of the known. The funny thing is that I work these things out back to front, as I get the inner knowing first and then I have to go and research certain topics so I can explain it in a manner that makes logical sense, as most of us have skepticism tendencies when it concerns matters that we don't fully understand. There's so much we don't fully understand.

In nature, ecosystems exhibit complex relationships between organisms and their environments, with each species playing a vital role in maintaining balance and showcasing a collective intelligence that sustains life through processes like pollination and nutrient cycling. Animal behaviour also reveals profound social structures: for instance, dolphins and elephants display deep emotional bonds and sophisticated communication, while ants and bees demonstrate remarkable co-operation and collective decision-making. In humans, our microbiome, composed of trillions of microorganisms interacts symbiotically with our bodies, influencing health, digestion, and even mood, highlighting the interconnectedness of our biology with other life forms. The concept of collective consciousness illustrates how shared beliefs and experiences shape cultures and societies, often leading to movements for social change. At a fundamental level, quantum physics uncovers interconnectedness at an atomic level, where phenomena like entanglement suggest that particles can influence one another instantaneously, hinting at deeper connections within the universe.

This awareness emphasises the importance of engaging in activities and goals that reflect our core values and passions, which enhances our sense of fulfilment and connection and overall equilibrium. While positive psychology highlights the benefits of pursuing what excites us, it's essential to consider the broader implications of our choices on our overall well-being and ensuring alignment with our purpose. This alignment reflects the adaptability of our minds, as seen in the field of neuroplasticity, which shows that we can evolve beyond our current states if we are willing to transcend the limits of the known, albeit a little tougher to do so when those neuropathways have already been established. Just as ecosystems showcase the complex relationships between organisms that maintain balance, our individual experiences contribute to the collective intelligence that sustains life as we know it.

Getting to know ourselves involves embracing all parts of our being, including those shaped by tragic or unjust experiences that may instill feelings such as hardship, pain, anger, deep sadness, shame, or guilt. This journey can be particularly challenging in the wake of unimaginable tragedies or crimes, where feelings of grief and injustice can feel overwhelmingly brutal. Acknowledging these aspects allows us to see reality as it truly is in the present moment, free from distortion. Accepting these difficult experiences can be viewed as integral to the human journey, each contributing to the person we are today. By recognising and validating all experiences and corresponding feelings, whether they arise from personal struggles, societal injustices, or traumatic events, we create space for healing and growth which may be a journey in its own right. This process requires us to confront feelings of shame, guilt, and a profound sense of injustice without judgment, acknowledging them as part of the spectrum of human emotion that arises in response to trauma and loss. In doing so, we honour our complexities and integrate our past into a more authentic sense of self, ultimately paving the way for transformation and resilience. While it may be difficult to see these feelings as natural, they are valid parts of life that allow us to process our pain and reclaim our sense of self amidst profound suffering. This acceptance deepens our self-awareness and enhances our emotional resilience. When you see these emotions not as burdens but as opportunities for insight and self-discovery, you cultivate a more nuanced understanding of your journey and ultimately of your very being. Acknowledging even the most uncomfortable moments fosters a sense of interconnectedness, as you come to realise that everyone faces their own struggles. This shared aspect of humanity enriches your relationships and fosters compassion for both yourself and others.

Ultimately, embracing the full spectrum of your feelings, not just the positive ones, allows us to live more authentically in the present and to be flagrantly ourselves for only then can we experience true connections, growth and the ability to connect with our authentic, higher selves. It enables us to appreciate the richness of life, understanding that even moments of difficulty are valuable parts of our growth and grand opportunities for our individual evolution. By welcoming all emotions into our experience, we deepen our connection to ourself and to the world around us, allowing us to navigate life with greater clarity and openness. Just don't forget to "release" them after they've served their purpose.

However, this does not mean acting impulsively on every emotion. Instead, it involves cultivating emotional intelligence and the ability to self-regulate during challenging moments, as per the 90 seconds suggested method by recognising your feelings without being overwhelmed by them or judging them, allowing yourself the opportunity to respond thoughtfully rather than react instinctively. The emotions really act as little sensors, guiding us towards our desired destination. By integrating self-awareness with emotional acceptance, you can navigate your experiences with greater resilience and clarity, leading to healthier choices and more meaningful connections. This balanced approach fosters a deeper understanding of your emotional landscape while promoting personal growth and well-being.

In our universe, everything occupies its own place, serves a specific function, and contributes to a harmonious whole, unless of course the balance is disrupted, and it is to a large extent, disrupted, globally. Cellphones for example disrupt our individual energy fields, over and above the radiation and all other scientifically proven damage, yet we all have one. We need to take a step back from elements that directly disrupt our energy fields and that's such a difficult challenge as we've become so reliant on using technology and our phones, but where there's a will, there's absolutely a way, at least for moderation. There's also the rise of materialism, superficiality, social media, big pharma, and consumer culture has increasingly diverted our attention from this natural equilibrium, from the way we were intended to be, in a state of inner peace and joyfulness, even in the face of challenges. The pursuit of power has been a fundamental aspect of human history, deeply rooted in our social structures, survival instincts, and cultural narratives. From ancient civilisations to modern societies, the desire for power has influenced human behaviour, relationships, and institutions. In early human communities, power often equated to access to resources such as food, shelter, and security. Those who held power could control these resources, ensuring their own survival and that of their group. As societies evolved, hierarchies emerged based on wealth, lineage, or military strength, intertwining the pursuit of power with social status. Cultural narratives, including myths and religious stories, have often glorified power, portraying leaders as heroic figures and embedding the idea that power is both desirable and noble. Psychologically, the pursuit of power is rooted in fundamental aspects of human nature. The need for control and influence stems from a desire for autonomy and self-efficacy, while fear of vulnerability and loss drives individuals to seek power as a means of establishing security. As inherently social beings, humans navigate power dynamics that shape relationships and interactions. The ability to influence others enhances one's sense of belonging and significance within a group. In contemporary society, the pursuit of power continues to manifest in various forms such as politics, corporate leadership, and social media influence - often leading to contested dynamics as marginalised groups challenge traditional power structures. Ultimately, this pursuit reflects our innate desires for security, status, and connection, driving human behaviour across time and cultures. Understanding it provides insights into current societal dynamics and the ongoing quest for power in all its forms.

The pervasive influence of advertising and technology, which uses psychological triggers and curated narratives, has many of us ensnared in cycles of consumption and mindless interactions, constantly seeking instant gratification that makes us "feel good" right now. Short term gains for long term suffering as we get distracted from what we could be focusing our attention on, i.e. the present moment, our goals and aspirations. For instance, how often do you find yourself scrolling through social media for hours, only to realise how much time has passed, or engaging in other distractions like binge-watching a TV series, reading the news or online shopping? Regardless of the distraction of your choice, and there is a wide range of options available nowadays, whether it's social media, news, or shopping, the result is the same: you are drawn further away from your true essence when not in moderation and used excessively. Don't tell me you have no time for yourself, to get fit, be it mentally or physically and then scroll online for hours on end, until your brain has numbed out and doesn't even register what it just encountered... This diversion serves the interests of those who design these platforms, as it leads to various desirable outcomes for them and simply put, it's good for business. Even the creators of these platforms openly acknowledge their addictive nature and their role in shaping our thoughts and behaviours, fully aware of how their designs exploit our psychological tendencies. This exposure to controlled narratives not only influences what we think but also distorts our perceptions of our desires and needs, disconnecting us from our true selves and leaving us in a constant state of scarcity, wanting more of what we don't really need, as we shift further away from internal balance and harmony.

In this journey of self-discovery, it's essential to be mindful of where and with whom we share our time and energy with. Friendships, like romantic relationships, hold immense power in shaping our sense of self. Surrounding ourselves with individuals who resonate with our values, beliefs, and spirit can deeply enrich our lives. These connections provide us with a sense of belonging and mutual understanding that is both grounding and uplifting.

Choosing a partner, for example: one who aligns with our essence, holds far more meaning than seeking attention or temporary satisfaction. While sensual exploration can be a beautiful way to understand and embrace the physical aspects of the body, pairing it with a spiritual connection elevates the experience, transforming it into something profoundly beautiful and fulfilling. Similarly, cultivating friendships based on authenticity, trust, and shared growth can lead to deeper emotional fulfillment, helping us navigate the complexities of life with greater wisdom and compassion.

The pursuit of immediate pleasure, whether physical or emotional, has driven a societal shift toward instant gratification. This relentless chase often overshadows the deeper aspects of life that contribute to genuine fulfilment. It's easy to become distracted by superficial markers of success, such as material possessions or fleeting relationships, often at the expense of our spiritual and emotional well-being. Similarly, engaging in casual or uncommitted relationships, or consuming adult content, which has been criticised for perpetuating unrealistic expectations and, in some cases, harmful industry practices, may offer temporary satisfaction but often leaves a sense of unfulfillment. These pursuits, though easily accessible and enticing, can hinder one's ability to address the deeper human need for meaningful connection, understanding, and purpose.

Intimacy, when grounded in authenticity and shared with a partner who aligns with our true self in the present moment, becomes a powerful act of love and growth. It's important to embrace this aspect of life not as a distraction, but as a reflection of the meaningful connections and spiritual depth we seek. Be patient and intentional when choosing a partner, ensuring they align with the energy and values you put out into the world. A meaningful relationship thrives on mutual respect, understanding, and shared intentions - it's not about simply settling for whoever comes along or allowing someone pushy to steer the relationship in their favour, especially someone more experienced than you. The right partner will complement your growth, honour your boundaries, and match your emotional investment. They won't coerce or manipulate to get their way but will instead collaborate with you to build a healthy, balanced connection. Waiting for someone who truly resonates with you might take time, but it's far better than rushing into something that doesn't align with your values or compromises your well-being. Remember, a relationship should enhance your life, not create imbalance or pressure. Trust the process, stay true to yourself, and have faith that the right person will come along when the time is right - someone who truly meets you where you are and values you for who you are. For now, for those that are not attached, just make sure you become the best version of yourself so you can attract a suitable partner into your life. I say all of that because I know from experience how easy it is to make the wrong decision, especially when you're young, naïve, and impressionable, with a biological clock ticking at the back of your head. In those moments, it's easy to be swayed by surface-level attraction or external pressures, rather than tuning into what truly aligns with your values and long-term goals. These mistakes can teach us valuable lessons, but they also highlight the importance of taking time to understand ourselves first and ensuring that any partner we choose is someone who genuinely supports and respects our journey. Rushing or settling often leads to complications that could have been avoided by waiting for the right connection to come along, and also accepting, that sometimes it won't and that is okay too.

Reconnecting with our authentic self involves moving beyond superficial desires and embracing a more profound understanding of our place in the universe. By focusing on what brings genuine joy and fostering authentic relationships, we align ourselves with our broader purpose. The first and most profound relationship we all need to engage in and fully invest ourselves in, is the one with ourselves. This shift requires intentional effort and the development of habits that support both personal and collective well-being. When we pursue our passions and align our actions with our values, we harmonise with the universe, leading to a sense of flow and ease in our lives.

To begin this journey of self-discovery and alignment, it's essential to carve out time for self-reflection, for quieting the mind and for formulating your desires. Regularly setting aside moments to connect with your aspirations and evaluate your path can help you understand the person you are and the person you aspire to be, should there be an element of misalignment. Making a plan and committing to it, regardless of your background or circumstances, is a powerful step towards achieving your goals. With the right mindset or attitude and dedication, you can overcome obstacles and realise your full potential, one little step at a time. When you still the mind, you allow yourself to experience the present moment in its purest form - unfiltered and unadulterated by distractions or preconceived notions. This state of mental clarity reveals the essence of the now, free from the excesses of past regrets or future anxieties. By quieting the internal noise, you cultivate a space where you can surrender to the present, approaching each moment with a sense of confidence, calmness and joy. This mindful presence not only enhances your appreciation for the simplicity and richness of each experience but also provides the clarity necessary for visualising and manifesting more of what you seek. When your mind is serene, you can envision your goals with greater purpose and focus, enabling you to manifest them more effectively. Thus, this state of inner stillness becomes a powerful foundation for achieving your aspirations, as it aligns your intentions with the clarity and purpose needed to bring them into reality.

You are capable of achieving absolutely anything that is real and aligned with the realm of possibility for your unique human experience. This doesn't mean you can become something you're not, like transforming into a different species or defying the laws of nature. Instead, it means that within the vast expanse of human potential, you hold the power to reach goals that align with your true abilities, passions, and purpose.

Whether it's mastering a skill, overcoming personal challenges, creating meaningful relationships, or contributing to the world in impactful ways, your capacity is limited only by your belief in yourself and the effort you're willing to invest. The quote from Anthony Trollope's Phineas Redux, "Difficult is done at once; the impossible takes a little longer," serves as a reminder that challenges and obstacles are not barriers but stepping stones to greatness. When you harness your willpower, determination, and creativity, you can accomplish extraordinary things - things that are real, meaningful, and entirely within your grasp as a human being.

While not everyone may have a specific set of aspirations or be ready to embark on a profound journey of transformation, it's important to understand that personal growth is a choice. If you seek transformation, regardless of its form, you have the ability to achieve it. Realising your desires requires self-honesty, commitment of time, and decisive action. This process begins with a willingness to challenge and alter the status quo, which necessitates consistency and intentional change, and starts with the active step of awareness.

For instance, adopting a healthier lifestyle might require you to reassess how you inter alia speak to yourself about food, establish earlier wake-up times, or make dietary changes - often involving the abandonment of ineffective habits. Through introspection, you can uncover the obstacles hindering your progress toward your goals or the version of yourself you aspire to be – you will know exactly what is standing in your way for as long as you are being honest with yourself. Addressing any issue in isolation will likely result in only temporary improvements, if at all, which is why many people give up when they don't see quick results and find the journey too challenging to maintain. True and lasting change necessitates a holistic approach, where every adjustment aligns with your overall objectives and fosters a more comprehensive and enduring transformation – there's no shortcuts I'm afraid and in most cases another "pill" is certainly not the answer. There are many professionals out there, from life coaches and psychologists to holistic practitioners, who can assist in this process, if you believe this is the way for you – there is no single way to achieve this and there is multiple ways to get to the same destination, however way you approach it though, you still need to put in the work, otherwise it's just knowing a bunch of stuff, theoretically speaking which has very little tangible value in your life if you don't apply it. Find out what you resonate with most, but remember that while external support can be valuable and offer guidance, the answers and peace you seek ultimately lie within you and you alone. You are more capable than you give yourself credit for!

Ultimately, personal growth involves addressing and overcoming the inner challenges that you have created or adopted over time. While this process may seem daunting, true transformation often occurs when you step outside your comfort zone. Embracing vulnerability and allowing yourself to make mistakes are essential parts of this journey. Through these experiences, you gain deeper self-awareness and understanding. It is crucial to practice self-compassion during this time and to refrain from comparing your progress with that of others, as each individual's journey is uniquely their own. Again, I am sharing my perspective, but you need to see what resonates with you and make it your own.

Maintaining focus on your personal path is essential for sustaining your energy and progress, keeping you grounded and balanced. This focus fosters a state of inner peace, enabling you to fully experience and embrace the full spectrum of emotions as they arise and pass through you. By nurturing this mindset, you create a supportive environment for meaningful and lasting personal growth, where self-discovery and transformation can truly flourish. Allow yourself to experience your feelings without rushing to label them as good or bad - emotions simply are what they are and they are all positive when they are justified. This acceptance helps you navigate your journey with greater authenticity and resilience.

What about our younger generation? Today's children, and I'm using the term "children" loosely to encompass youth of all ages, face significant challenges in an increasingly complex world. They are often socially stunted by the distractions of instant gratification from technology, media, and the easy accessibility of unhealthy foods and other indulgences. This phenomenon not only affects the children but also impacts their caregivers, diminishing the personal connection and engagement necessary for healthy development. Without this essential interpersonal connectivity, children may struggle to develop the neurological pathways needed to thrive, growing up with a profound sense of lack. This gap in social skills and connectedness, both within the home and in society at large, heightens the risk of harmful coping mechanisms, feelings of inadequacy and purposelessness, as well as a full wide range of mental illnesses. These can take the form of substance abuse, self-harm, or other destructive behaviours, often used as an escape from unresolved and overwhelming emotions they have not been equipped to process and deal with. Rather than focusing solely on unlearning harmful habits, it's crucial to guide children toward appreciating their unique contributions and recognising the interconnectedness of all things. This positive approach fosters a deep sense of purpose and belonging, empowering them to live lives filled with dignity and joy. With this foundation, they can navigate the complexities of the world in healthier, more meaningful ways, reducing their reliance on quick fixes and building resilience for the future. Here I would like to highlight the Rat Park experiment, which was designed to challenge and re-evaluate earlier studies on drug addiction (which is a massive global problem, and I say problem, because it just shows you how many people are struggling with themselves and use it as a copying mechanism) that used isolated and barren environments for rats. In these earlier experiments, rats were placed in small, individual cages with access to a water solution containing morphine. The results consistently showed that these rats developed addictive behaviours towards the morphine-laced water, leading to the conclusion that the drugs themselves were inherently addictive. Skeptical of these findings,

Bruce Alexander, a Canadian psychologist, conducted his own experiment in the 1970's. He questioned whether the isolated and stressful conditions of the previous studies were influencing the results. Alexander proposed that addiction might be more closely related to environmental and social factors than to the pharmacological properties of the drugs themselves. To test this hypothesis, he created Rat Park, a spacious, enriched environment where rats could socialise, play, and explore. In this setting, rats had the choice between plain water and morphine-laced water. The results were striking: rats in Rat Park were much less likely to self-administer the morphine compared to those in isolated cages. This finding suggested that a supportive and stimulating environment significantly reduced the likelihood of addictive behaviour, highlighting the role of social and environmental factors in addiction and challenging the notion that drugs are solely responsible for addiction.

For younger generations to thrive and build healthy relationships with themselves and others, it is essential that they are grounded in fundamental universal truths and equipped with the right tools for personal development, self-awareness, self-regulation, and goal-setting. Embracing and integrating these principles from an early age can profoundly influence their path toward a fulfilling and balanced life, helping them navigate challenges with greater clarity and purpose. Not all children are fortunate enough to grow up in a loving and emotionally stable homes with balanced parental figures. In such cases, the only other environment that can provide a consistent and nurturing foundation is the school system. Schools have the potential to offer not only education but also emotional safety, guidance, and a sense of belonging, which are critical for a child's emotional and psychological development. When teachers, mentors, and peers model empathy, patience, and emotional regulation, children who lack this at home can still experience what healthy connection and support feel like. This becomes essential for shaping their self-worth, emotional intelligence, and ability to build meaningful relationships later in life. In this sense, schools have the power to fill the emotional gaps that many children carry, helping them break generational cycles and develop into balanced, emotionally aware adults. However, for this to happen, the current education system would need to evolve beyond academics and place more focus on emotional intelligence, self-awareness, and mental well-being. This requires a fundamental shift in the way we approach human development - one that recognises that education is not just about the mind, but also about the heart and the soul. It's not merely about intellectual knowledge; it's about understanding the emotional landscape, how the mind works, and how we process and respond to our inner and outer worlds. True education must address not only the development of cognitive skills but also the emotional intelligence, resilience, and self-awareness that allow individuals to navigate life with balance and depth.

Firstly, embracing the idea that personal growth involves confronting and overcoming inner challenges is essential. These challenges, whether self-imposed or adopted from external influences, are part of the journey to self-discovery and transformation. Stepping outside one's comfort zone, though often daunting, is where true growth and change occur. Encouraging young people to embrace vulnerability, allowing them to make mistakes without being shamed or judged, and learning from them fosters resilience and a deeper understanding of themselves.

Practicing self-compassion is equally important. Young individuals should be taught to be kind to themselves during their journey, recognising that setbacks and imperfections are natural aspects of personal development and ultimately, being human. Avoiding comparisons with others is crucial, as each person's path is unique. Comparison is the thief of joy of the present moment and the root of later perceptions which can take one on a downward spiral. This focus on individual progress, on the present moment, helps maintain energy and motivation, and supports a balanced, grounded approach to life.

Additionally, understanding that emotions are neither inherently good nor bad, but simply part of the human experience, is vital. Encouraging young people to fully experience their emotions, teaching them the 90 seconds lifespan of emotions, without rushing to categorise them promotes emotional intelligence and resilience. This approach helps them navigate their feelings with authenticity and balance, contributing to overall well-being.

A holistic approach to personal development is also beneficial. Being mindful of the food they consume, being physically active and seeking mental growth. Young people should be further encouraged to adopt practices that align with their values and goals, such as mindfulness, self-reflection, and goal setting. Seeking guidance from their educators, which too need to be educated on the topic, can provide valuable support, but it is important to remember that the most profound answers and insights often come from within. We need to teach the youth to trust their inner knowing and how in the world could they ever do that, if we don't demonstrate that?

Finally, fostering a strong sense of purpose and vision is crucial. Young individuals should be encouraged to explore their passions and set meaningful goals, as a clear sense of purpose helps maintain focus and motivation while providing direction through life's challenges. It's important to approach this journey with an open mind and avoid making judgments - support and understanding are essential as they navigate their path. By embracing their unique journey without judgment, they can cultivate a more authentic and fulfilling life experience, leading to a more joyful way of being and living and they won't have as many layers to peel as they grow older or will be better equipped to do so and can transcend to another level of consciousness. Sparking curiosity and self-reflection.

The moment you realise that everything you've ever wanted and needed lies within you, albeit not perfect, is the moment you'll liberate yourself from the inner tyrant who's continuously pushing you towards uncertainty, dissatisfaction and the feeling of lack, who's so easily able to sway your beliefs and thoughts in whichever direction your distraction lies and ultimately take your joy away through doubt, comparison, jealousy or greed. When I say something is not perfect, I mean that "perfection" is often a subjective concept rooted in perceived idealism - the belief that things should meet an imagined or unattainable standard. Perfection, in this sense, suggests that something or someone is not as they "should" be, according to a particular set of expectations or ideals. However, these ideals are shaped by personal experiences, societal pressures, or cultural norms, making perfection a moving target. What one person perceives as "perfect" may not resonate with another, because what is truly perfect is often about accepting things as they are, imperfections included. Rather than striving for an impossible ideal, embracing what is can lead to a deeper appreciation of what is unique and valuable in any given moment or person. The moment you find the answer of who it is that you are, and what is your essence, nothing and no one can stand in your way but you, for you will get to know all of you, the value that you add, whilst standing firmly unphased in the face of adversity, confidently knowing that you can overcome any challenge that may present itself, even the unthinkable kind, for as long as you stay true to yourself and the natural flow of life, and you do so with integrity. Be flagrantly you, whilst maintaining mindfulness, and don't make yourself smaller than you are for anybody, don't accept being mistreated in any shape or form, do not allow anyone to put you in a situation where you feel pressured to compromise on your values or make poor choices and don't be afraid to take some action towards your vision, which will inevitably be hard work. Educate yourself in your field of interest. Remember that whatever beliefs you carry, will be reaffirmed, so be sure to be truly yourself at all times so you can attract your tribe of like-minded individuals, who'll help you reaffirm your beliefs and help you reach your goals in life, for although we need to know ourselves and do the best for ourselves, we are also a part of a bigger picture and part of a collective.

Let's make this a movement aimed at the betterment of society and a way of life, by equipping the younger generations with true value, a sense of self and a sense of purpose. This initiative might be the start of something transformative, sparking conversations as a start. By integrating these principles into their lives, younger generations will be better equipped to build healthy relationships with themselves and others, and to navigate life's challenges with resilience, and achieve personal fulfilment.

4 A METAMORPHOSIS KIND OF TRANSFORMATION

At some point in our lives, before the weight of societal expectations creeped in and embedded themselves upon us, before we unconsciously absorbed the habits and worldviews of our caregivers, the media or other sources of influence, we each embodied the pure wonder and boundless imagination of childhood. We were like pawns on a chessboard, innocent and unaware of the vast potential within us. Just as a pawn may appear small and limited, its journey across the board reveals a transformative truth: it has the power to become a queen, the piece that commands the game, shapes strategy, and changes outcomes. In the same way, we are more than what meets the eye and a part of a vast, powerful universe brimming with possibility. Imagine for a moment the innocence of childhood games, like hide and seek. The thrill of hiding, the exhilaration of being found, or the moment of discovery - these weren't just fleeting joys. They mirrored the chessboard's magic, where every move invites exploration, strategy, and the anticipation of uncovering something extraordinary. In those moments, ordinary spaces became enchanted realms, and the act of play grounded us fully in the present, a place where possibility felt infinite. To embrace our inner child is to look into the mirror, much like the pawn gazing back to see its reflection as a queen. It is to recognise that the playful, imaginative spirit still lives within us, quietly longing to reconnect, express, and transform. Life, like the chessboard, invites us to take bold steps, to explore, and to awaken to the truth of our power. It reminds us that no matter where we come from or how complex our paths to date, we are all capable of running the board and calling the shots, creating connection, and embodying the fullness of who we truly are. I love speaking in game terms as I love to play games, although over the years I have transitioned to more strategy orientated board games.

The concept of the inner child refers to the part of our being that retains the emotional experiences, memories, and needs from our early childhood, some of which may have been met, some of which were not and some of which may have been suppressed, as that is what we do best – we find a way to endure and persevere, albeit not always in the most beneficial ways, as we create biases and patterns that shape our adult lives. These coping mechanisms, born from unmet needs or overwhelming experiences, can serve us in the moment but may lead to maladaptive behaviours later on. By recognising and nurturing our inner child, we can start to unpack these biases and understand their origins, and then let them go if they no longer serve us, as discussed in the previous chapter. This journey enables us to validate those early emotions and experiences, integrate them into our self-awareness, and cultivate the compassion needed to navigate life more constructively. This, in turn, empowers us to make conscious decisions about whether we want to change in any particular way and take action accordingly. I know how scary changes can seem, but changes mean transformation and growth, which is what we want. Get excited about it, it's bloody exciting!

Look at the transformation of a caterpillar into a butterfly-what a powerful symbol of change and growth, also known as metamorphosis. I believe there's many symbolic similarities of the various stages that we go through, which resonate with that of a caterpillar. It all begins with the female butterfly laying eggs on a suitable host plant, representing potential and new beginnings. Once the eggs hatch, the caterpillar emerges, entering a phase characterised by voracious feeding and rapid growth. As it consumes leaves, the caterpillar symbolises the importance of nourishment and learning during times of change, shedding its skin multiple times as it outgrows its form. After reaching a certain size, it forms a protective chrysalis around itself, where it undergoes a remarkable transformation. Inside, the caterpillar breaks down its larval body, reorganising into a butterfly, which represents introspection and the often uncomfortable process of change. Finally, when the chrysalis splits open, the butterfly emerges with crumpled, damp wings that eventually dry and expand, allowing it to fly. This stage symbolises freedom, beauty, and the culmination of personal growth, reminding us that transformation often requires patience, adaptation, overcoming challenges and a willingness to embrace the unknown, which may appear dark and scary. Just as the caterpillar doesn't resist its transformation but surrenders to an innate, intelligent process, we too can learn to embrace our personal metamorphosis. The caterpillar doesn't fight against becoming a butterfly: it trusts the inherent wisdom of its biological programming. Similarly, our personal transformation requires a similar surrender - not to external forces, but to our own inner potential. The chrysalis isn't a moment of weakness, but a profound period of internal reorganisation, where what seems like dissolution is actually the most creative moment of rebirth.

Going back to the inner child has its significance in that it really represents our formative experiences, both positive and negative (although I try and stay away from labels), and can influence our emotional responses and behaviours in adulthood and often do, sometimes without us even realising this. Healing the inner child involves recognising and addressing these early emotional wounds/traumas in order to foster personal growth and emotional well-being, which starts with bringing awareness to the way we react and feel in certain circumstances which we find triggering. Ask yourself, "Why am I being triggered here?". At this point, you need to be brutally honest with yourself - drop the victimhood mentality and take ownership of whatever surfaces. Don't look to blame others for making you feel a certain way. Instead, try to genuinely identify the reason behind the emotional trigger.

Sometimes the cause isn't obvious, and in such cases, you can ask yourself a slightly different question: "What is it that I have to believe is true in order to feel this way?". No one can make you feel a particular way unless a part of you resonates with it, fears that others might believe it, or believes what they're saying, even if it isn't true at all. Emotional responses are very often tied to underlying core beliefs or stories we tell ourselves and unresolved issues. For example, if your partner's comment triggers feelings of inadequacy, it may be linked to your own deep-rooted insecurities, which often take root in early childhood. These insecurities stem from core beliefs or subconscious ideas we hold about ourselves and the world, which are shaped by our earliest experiences. Perhaps, as a child, you felt unseen, unheard, or judged, and over time, you internalised beliefs like: "I'm not good enough" or "I have to prove my worth to be accepted or loved."

Similarly, if someone calls you a liar or spreads a rumour about you that isn't true, the reason it affects you so deeply might be tied to an unresolved core belief. For instance, you might unconsciously fear that others will believe the lie, which could trigger feelings of shame or rejection. This reaction might stem from a childhood experience where your truth was dismissed, you were unfairly blamed, or your integrity was questioned. These moments left an imprint, creating a vulnerability to similar situations in adulthood.

To effectively handle such triggers, start by identifying these core beliefs and reflecting on recurring emotional patterns. Ask yourself: "Why does this hurt me so much?", "What past experiences does this remind me of?". Recognising these patterns allows you to respond with awareness rather than reacting impulsively. It's also crucial to acknowledge that feeling triggered is a natural part of the human experience. It doesn't define your worth or reflect a lack of strength. Triggers are opportunities for growth - signposts guiding you toward the unresolved parts of yourself that long for healing. By addressing the root of these beliefs, you can gradually free yourself from their hold and step into a more grounded and empowered version of yourself, which is your authentic self.

The idea behind unpacking your past and working with your inner child involves exploring childhood experiences, feelings, and beliefs that have shaped who you are today. Unresolved issues from childhood can significantly influence your emotions, behaviours, and relationships in adulthood. By addressing these past experiences, you can better understand patterns in your life, recognising how they affect your current behaviours and identifying those that no longer serve you and working on letting them go by changing the very beliefs that keeps them active or in other words, addressing the story we have been telling ourselves and have accepted as truth. This process also allows you to heal emotional wounds by acknowledging and processing painful memories, leading to greater emotional resilience. Additionally, connecting with your inner child fosters self-compassion, enabling you to nurture and support the vulnerable parts of yourself, which ultimately cultivates self-love and acceptance. As you integrate these past experiences, you develop a clearer sense of identity and purpose, empowering personal growth and healthier relationships. Overall, this journey promotes self-awareness and emotional well-being, allowing you to live more authentically.

To avoid falling into a victimhood mentality, you can take

ownership of your emotional responses. This means acknowledging that while you may not have control over others' actions, you do have control over how you react, irrespective of the severity of the circumstances. Instead of jumping at the opportunity to blame others for the way they made you feel, how they disrespected you or otherwise hurt your feelings or how they took advantage of your kind nature or physically caused you pain and suffering, try to understand that your responses are influenced by your own interpretations and beliefs about the situation and in most circumstances have nothing to do with the other person.

Emotions are just energy in motion – signals that arise from within, often rooted in subconscious patterns and belief systems we've carried for years (or even generations). They aren't "good" or "bad", but they simply point us toward something that needs attention, healing, or release. When we suppress or ignore emotions, they don't disappear, but instead they get stored in the body as tension, discomfort, or even illness. But when we allow ourselves to feel them fully, without judgment, we can begin to understand the belief systems that created them in the first place. The beauty is that once we become aware of these internal signals, we can start to shift those beliefs, rewire old patterns, and ultimately free ourselves from emotional cycles that no longer serve us.

The body is always speaking, and it's just a matter of whether we're willing to listen. We can practice cognitive-behavioural techniques ("CBT") to challenge and reframe cognitive distortions such as all-or-nothing thinking or personalisation, which can exacerbate emotional reactions. One of the core techniques is identifying cognitive distortions. These are biased ways of thinking that can exaggerate negative feelings. For instance, if you think "I always mess things up" after a small mistake, you're engaging in all-or-nothing kind of thinking. By recognising such distortions, you can challenge and reframe them.

Another common belief I, too, was guilty of holding onto was "I am not good enough." From an early age, I often felt inadequate, especially when compared to other kids who seemed to do better in certain things - those who got higher marks at school or displayed the qualities I seemingly did not display at the markers my mother would have liked me to. My older sister, a straight-A student, was a constant reminder of what I thought I was missing, while I barely scraped through high school as I just hated it so much on an emotional level. No matter how much effort I put in, it never seemed to measure up, so I just stopped putting in the effort. This relentless comparison, I now realise, is the thief of joy, slowly chipping away at self-worth.

When we begin to diminish our own value, the world mirrors that belief back to us. As creators of our own realities, what we focus on internally will be reaffirmed externally, shaping the way we experience life. Yet, alongside this implanted doubt, there was also a part of me that had an unshakable vision. Even as a child, I had a very particular taste that gravitated toward quality. I remember my mother's words vividly, telling me that I couldn't exceed my capabilities or the family's existing means. My response was always the same: "I can't help myself. I have a vision, and I strive for bigger things, even if they are beyond my reach right now." Back then, I technically had no means at all - I was dependent on my parents, but I couldn't ignore the pull toward something greater, something beyond my current reality.

Still, beneath that bold vision lay a deep longing to feel accepted and appreciated for who I was. I sought my mother's constant approval, wanting her to recognise and affirm my unique qualities. When that validation didn't come in the ways I needed it to, it left me feeling like I wasn't enough as I was. Over time, this created a sense of lack, not because I wasn't capable or deserving, but because I tied my worth to external acknowledgment.

As the years went by, this belief in my inadequacy grew or was rather reaffirmed. The confident belief in my potential wavered, replaced by doubt. I began to think that achieving great success or experiencing true happiness might not be "on the cards" for me. I became overly concerned with meeting the expectations of others. I'd often say "yes" to things I didn't want to do, hoping to gain validation or recognition, only to realise that this effort was rarely reciprocated. I was seeking love, approval, and worthiness outside of myself, not understanding that these were things only I could cultivate from within.

Looking back, I now understand that these feelings of inadequacy and doubt were shaped by deeply embedded experiences, not objective truths. As children, we absorb messages from our surroundings - comments, comparisons, and limitations - and these form our core beliefs. For me, the belief that "I'm not good enough" emerged not only from being compared to others but also from my yearning for approval, particularly from my mother.

But here's the empowering truth: these beliefs are not facts. They are stories we tell ourselves, often unconsciously, and the good news is that we have the power to rewrite them. It doesn't have to be this way.

What's even more striking is that these stories we create are often far from the truth. In conversations with my mother, for instance, she has been genuinely shocked by how I felt. What I perceived as criticism or pressure was, in her mind, an effort to encourage me and help me reach my full potential. This revelation transformed my understanding of those childhood experiences. It wasn't that she thought I wasn't good enough - she simply wanted me to recognize my own capabilities, though her approach unintentionally reinforced my insecurities.

I share this because it highlights the importance of avoiding the projection of our own insecurities and belief systems onto others, especially our children. As parents, caregivers, or role models, our role isn't to mold them into something they're not but to love, support, and nurture them as they are. How we feel and the love we feel needs to translate in a manner that is felt, as often there is that disconnect, which causes problems later on in life. When we attempt to change their essence, we risk saddling them with a lifetime of unravelling what was never theirs to carry in the first place. This is the cycle of generational trauma - a pattern we can break by fostering acceptance, understanding, and unconditional love. By challenging these old narratives and cultivating self-worth from within, we can free ourselves from the trap of comparison and the need for external validation. The vision I held as a child, which is that pull toward something greater, was always a part of me. It was never about having the means at the time, but about recognising that I was capable of more, even if I couldn't yet see how. Reconnecting with that belief and honouring it today has been a transformative reminder that "I am enough" just as I am, and so are you.

Our brains are not necessarily designed to see the entire path forward in a linear way, but rather to address things as they surface in the present moment. The brain is highly adaptive and equipped to focus on immediate challenges, processing information and reacting to it based on past experiences, emotions, and survival instincts. This is often referred to as "reactive thinking," where the brain prioritises responding to stimuli as they arise. At the same time, the brain does have the ability to anticipate future scenarios, plan ahead, and set long-term goals, which is more aligned with "proactive thinking." This is where our capacity for foresight, decision-making, and planning comes into play. However, even in the case of proactive thinking, we tend to focus on one step at a time, processing new information as it becomes relevant, and adjusting our plans based on the circumstances that unfold. In essence, while our brains have the ability to visualise the future and set goals, they are wired to address challenges and process information in a way that allows us to react to the present moment. It's the balance of both reactive and proactive thinking that helps us navigate life, allowing us to stay grounded while also preparing for what lies ahead.

The more we avoid introspection and looking inwards, the deeper we sink into the quicksand of negative beliefs about ourselves and our circumstances, and we end up stuck in this rat race of daily chores and responsibilities without the capacity or willingness for introspection. We start believing that our present situation is the status quo and that we are incapable of breaking the mold. This spiral can feel inescapable, reinforcing feelings of inadequacy and self-doubt. However, change begins with a single step. Start today, even if it's small.

Take a moment each day to pause and reflect on your thoughts and feelings – I do this every single day and definitely before bedtime, as it's a guaranteed and consistent time for me to do so. I also love writing down any beliefs I want to challenge as well as any epiphanies that flow through me in the form of inner knowing's. Epiphanies can feel like a powerful rush of insight or clarity that flows through you, often bringing a sense of awakening or realisation, which comes with a strong sense of knowing. They can emerge unexpectedly, sometimes triggered by a moment of reflection, a conversation, or even an everyday experience – I am a firm believer that those that seek, they find just what they seek. When this happens, it's as if everything clicks into place, revealing new perspectives and understandings. This flow of realisation can be energising and transformative, encouraging you to reframe your beliefs and embrace change. Being open to these moments can enrich your journey of self-discovery and growth.

Practice mindfulness, allowing yourself to observe your thoughts without judgment. Instead of criticising yourself with questions like: "How did I allow myself to be treated this way?" or "How could I not see this?" try reframing them. Ask yourself: "What can I learn from this experience?" or "How can I grow from what happened?". Set aside time for self-compassion, treating yourself as you would someone you love, recognising that everyone has their own little quirks and everyone makes mistakes and that's all part of the learning process. By taking these small steps toward self-reflection and acceptance, you can gradually shift your mindset and break free from the cycle of your daily routine or negative thought patterns, fostering a healthier and more positive self-image, choosing a pathway towards authentic way of living.

Reframing your thoughts involves shifting your perspective on a situation, which can only come from a place of awareness. For example, instead of viewing a minor criticism as a personal failure, you might reframe it as an opportunity for growth – I like to call that kind of shift: paying your "school fees", as often these lessons come at a cost. I've paid many school fees to date and I am sure there's still lots to pay, but I have learnt that everything can be perfect on paper and still go wrong, especially when you are not in tune with yourself. I have learnt that not all people mean well and some are willing to compromise who they are to get ahead, but then I have also learnt to recognise those that have strong and healthy values and ethics – know who you are dealing with, listen to your inner knowing and do not judge a book by its cover, unless it's mine, in which case do go ahead as a lot of thought went into that. I have also learnt that things are often not as scary as we make them out to be and the more desperately we want something to work out, the more likely it is that it will slip away. Choosing dysfunctional relationships because they remind you of what "home" felt like for you, or because your biological clock is ticking is nothing more than fear of rejection, and fear of the unknown or failure to meet societal pressures, paired with the disbelief that you deserve better. Well, you do. You deserve better than that, so don't go and drop your standards of what you are inherently meant for.

Another useful CBT technique is keeping thought records, which can be in the form of keeping a diary, where you get to capture your thoughts in particular situations and how you responded or how you wish you responded. Here it is good to be aware that some people are better than others at thinking fast on their feet and the articulation that follows, and some people need a minute before they respond in a particular situation (even me, and I am pretty good at thinking fast on my feet) and if that is the case, bring awareness to it, and when a situation arises where a fast response is required that you feel uncertain about (possibly because your emotions are heightened), don't be afraid to say: "I need some time to consider what you are saying and I will get back to you." and request a reasonable time to do so. You can do this at any time, even a job interview where you feel unprepared to answer a question – ask for a moment to just collect your thoughts. I have done this in the middle of meetings too, so don't be afraid to ask for a moment to either center yourself or just better consider your options, whatever the case may be. You don't have to have the answer on the spot each time.

Write down the situation, your emotional response, and the thoughts you had. Then, analyse these thoughts to identify distortions and come up with more balanced alternatives. For instance, if you're feeling anxious about something or have imposter thoughts running through your mind, note down the thoughts that may be fuelling your anxiety and then challenge these thoughts with evidence that supports your capabilities, bearing in mind that we were all beginners at some point in any task we embark on. We are all capable to push beyond the known, beyond our limitations and to reinforce our sense of self and potential.

Behavioural experiments also play a key role in CBT technique. This involves testing out your beliefs through small, controlled experiments, in practice. For example, if you believe that asking for help will make you seem weak or rather, unskilled, try asking for assistance on a minor task and observe the outcome. Often, these experiments reveal that our fears are very much exaggerated and through practice, help us adjust our beliefs based on real experiences. I am also a firm believer that if you do not ask, you will not receive in life. Seek assistance and answers to questions you may have and do so thoughtfully and respectfully, ensuring you don't exploit the generosity or kind nature of others. Sometimes we just need another perspective to help us reaffirm our own, until we learn to trust ourselves a little more.

By applying these simple CBT techniques, identifying cognitive distortions, reframing negative thoughts, using thought records, and conducting behavioural experiments -you can gain better control over your emotional responses, as you get to alter your own beliefs and this in turn will reduce the impact of triggers, and transform your current state of being.

These CBT techniques work particularly well when integrated

with inner child work. As you identify cognitive distortions, you may discover that many stem from childhood experiences where your inner child formed beliefs about safety, worth, or belonging. When journaling or keeping thought records, consider writing with your non-dominant hand occasionally to access younger, less filtered thoughts from your inner child. During behavioral experiments, notice which situations trigger childlike reactions of fear or insecurity - these are opportunities to nurture your inner child while creating new, empowering experiences for your adult self.

In addition to the CBT techniques aforementioned, there's ways for you to protect yourself while remaining vulnerable, which involves amongst other things setting healthy boundaries and developing emotional resilience, which of course comes with practice and just knowing yourself to the core. I used to think that showing my vulnerable side is a sign of weakness as this would mean exposing those parts of me which can be hurt, but as it turns out, this is where my strength lies and nobody can hurt me without my permission. Permission not granted! Boundaries are crucial for safeguarding your emotional well-being while still allowing you to be receptive and authentic – have some boundaries and don't be rigid about all of them, remain a level of flexibility and recognise that those boundaries will likely evolve with time. Clearly define what behaviours are acceptable and what is absolutely not acceptable, and communicate these boundaries assertively, but with empathy. Building emotional resilience through mindfulness and emotional regulation techniques, such as deep breathing and grounding exercises, helps you stay centered and respond to triggers more thoughtfully.

Maintaining vulnerability requires discernment. Share your authentic self with those who have demonstrated trustworthiness and respect, ensuring that your openness does not expose you to unnecessary harm. For this, you cannot rush things, relationships and your openness prematurely would be quite frankly a little dicey, as not everyone has your best interests at heart and you need to be in a position and give yourself the time necessary to find more about the other person standing in front of you, to find out what they are all about, to listen to your inner knowing and to observe their actions, for I am a firm believer that actions speak louder than words. Foster relationships with individuals who honour your boundaries and provide a safe space for vulnerability. This balance allows you to remain true to yourself while protecting your emotional safety.

Building emotional intelligence is about strengthening your ability to recognise and manage your emotions without getting stuck in them. For many, this looks less like journaling and more like engaging in actions that create mental clarity - whether that's through physical activity, working on a project of sorts, or simply taking time in nature. Another powerful tool is changing the way you speak to yourself. Instead of harsh self-criticism, try giving yourself the kind of advice or support you'd offer a close friend. Reward yourself for wins, even small ones, and allow yourself to rest without feeling the need to "earn it" or allowing yourself to enjoy something you've been wanting without guilt. You don't have to talk about emotions to process them, but when you start showing up for yourself with respect and kindness, it naturally shifts how you handle challenges and connect with others. These are just little examples and suggestions, but you need to figure out what would work out best for you, and that's rather fun.

By integrating these approaches, you can effectively manage emotional triggers, protect your well-being, and maintain your authenticity in relationships. This ongoing process requires continuous self-reflection, adjustment, and growth, enabling you to navigate your emotional landscape with greater clarity and strength. Be patient with yourself – it's a work in progress and what matters the most is that with each passing day, you are a little wiser and a little kinder to yourself and those around you.

Having said all of that, we have all been subjected to some or other degree to the ways of our parents, care givers, our peers, our educators etc, be it by the words spoken to us or as a result of our observation of the way those people conducted themselves, which may or may not coincide with our own belief system, and having said that I have not yet met a person that upon reflection does not recognise that they have adopted, along with the good some of the not so good or rather non-beneficial habits from a number of people, but possibly the care givers being the primary source, which is not exactly the easiest to shake off, especially if you are not equipped with the knowledge and skill to do so. It has been a struggle for me too, to shake off what I have observed, especially in my interactions with others, for my parents are not exactly the most patient people and have many of their own personal battles and run away from confrontation about topics that are sensitive to them. They also battle to speak up when their feelings get hurt or someone crosses their boundary (which leads to the topic of knowing yourself and what your personal boundaries are) and at some point, you witness an outburst that makes no sense to you. In my family when I was a child, the go to has always been to sweep conflict under the rug, and swiftly move on, which naturally resulted in plenty of unnecessary verbal outbursts, a lot of slammed doors, feelings of anger and resentment at times within the family unit, snappiness and more often than not, such felt to be without merit as there is also a lot of love, but I guess conflict is a little bit like a pressure cooker, the steam build-up needs to be released one way or another and if not done in a safe manner with intent, care and consideration, we're looking at potential explosion and a 4th degree burn.

Just as a pressure cooker has safety mechanisms to release excess steam, we need healthy outlets and coping strategies to manage our own emotions effectively. By acknowledging our feelings, communicating openly and empathetically, and addressing issues constructively, we can maintain emotional balance and prevent overwhelming pressure from causing harm – you can't take back words or unhear them either.

Acknowledge how you feel and remember that healing can only begin when you acknowledge the presence of the inner child and when you actively connect with this aspect of yourself. This involves reflecting on past experiences and understanding how they shape your current behaviours and emotional responses.

Generally speaking, our behaviours and emotional responses in turn can lead to some or other form of conflict, disagreement or misunderstanding unless we have already mastered the art of self-regulating ourselves to the point where nothing and no one can phase us and deviate us from our own path, which naturally comes with knowing oneself fully. As a legal practitioner, I have learnt all about conflict and how to deal with it and I will share my know how in that regard, for I believe that it is not only effective but necessary to know. Conflict resolution is not only about having good negotiation skills and being able to compromise, but it is also about having a deep understanding of the person's emotions and their motivation, alongside your own. What I believe to be the first most important step is to ensure that you are calm and clear with your own intentions and what you are trying to achieve when entering any discussions and that your responses are calm and if triggered and you feel yourself losing composure, rather take some time to calm yourself down before resuming discussions – it takes approximately 90 seconds for the emotion to run its course, if unentertained. It is also very important to ensure that you hear the other side out, and really and actively hear them out and their perspective, so as to better assess such, consider alongside your own and find common ground, which is fair for both parties. This approach ensures not only effective conflict resolution, but also that such is reached in a mutually respective manner, both in terms of values and interests. Here there is a strong element of inner dialogue, some of which needs to be with your inner child, in order to find out what is the reason behind your triggers and so as to enable yourself to be set free of such, by offering yourself the same level of compassion, understanding and support, that you'd offer a loved one, and what I find very helpful during such exploration is taking notes. You do not need to be good at it and everybody is capable of it - the moment you seek an answer, such will present itself at the right time. Be receptive and open to receive the answers.

Allow yourself the chance to express your emotions that may have been suppressed or that remain unacknowledged. This can involve expressing grief, anger, or joy that your inner child might have missed out on, holds onto or struggled with in the past. Allow this emotion to pass through you and just set it free, for emotions are not meant to be held onto, but rather acknowledged for the reason they arose within us and released the moment they have served their purpose.

Allowing emotions to pass through us and setting them free involves recognising that emotions are temporary and should not be clung to or suppressed. When we experience them fully but without attachment, we honor their message while preventing them from becoming entrenched patterns that impact our long-term mental health. Emotions naturally arise in response to specific triggers and often dissipate after a short period. Understanding this impermanence helps manage emotions effectively without letting them dominate our mental state or the way we conduct ourselves.

When we experience an emotion, it's important to fully

acknowledge and experience it without judgment. For example, if you feel sadness, recognise it as such and observe how it manifests in your body and mind. This acknowledgment helps in processing the emotion rather than being overwhelmed by it and wishing it away. Let it stay and run its course, consciously.

Once you've recognised and experienced the emotion, focus on releasing it, for it has served its purpose. This can be achieved through practices like mindfulness, journaling, or talking with someone you trust – whatever it is that works for you. Mindfulness involves observing the emotion as it arises and then letting it drift away, similar to watching a cloud move across the sky and transform in shape or form as the wind blows it over. Journaling allows you to express and then distance yourself from the emotion, while talking it out with someone can provide perspective and emotional relief. When responding to communication that triggers frustration, which can happen frequently in the legal field where mind games are common, I've found it helpful to draft my response initially but hold off on sending it. I then take time to revise my message when I'm in a calmer state. The version I ultimately send is often quite different from my initial draft. Something to keep in mind when triggered.

Avoiding emotional cling is crucial, as holding onto negative emotions can lead to chronic stress and anxiety, amongst other things. For instance, persistently reliving a traumatic event, such as the loss of a loved one, can exacerbate your suffering rather than aid in healing. It's important to recognise that clinging to grief or negative feelings does not bring the person back nor does it reflect the depth of your love for them. The idea that prolonged grieving is a measure of how much you loved someone is a misconception. Grieving is a natural process, but it should not be confused with maintaining a constant state of distress. Instead, allowing yourself to move through grief and eventually find acceptance can be a more profound way to honour the memory of a loved one while also caring for your own emotional well-being. Holding onto negative emotions does not enhance the significance of your relationship but rather can hinder your ability to heal and find peace.

Similarly, holding onto positive emotions too tightly brings about a similar result, as you may develop unrealistic expectations or pressures to continually feel the exact same way. This can lead to anxiety and disappointment if those feelings inevitably change or fluctuate, which is natural to be the case. You basically rob yourself from the natural flow of emotions which enable you to remain adaptable, grounded, and fully engaged with your present experiences. In essence, emotions are meant to flow through us, and by releasing them, we maintain emotional balance and well-being. Another thing to remember is that all emotions are positive for as long as they are appropriate and are afforded the opportunity to run their natural course.

Insofar as healthy outlets and coping strategies are concerned, you need to look within and find out what is the thing that helps you stay calm, collected and clear – what is the thing that helps you regain control and composure. More often than not, through practice, I find that I am able to regain control through my inner dialogue as I pick up immediately when there is a shift in my emotional state and I ensure that I address it, in a way that does not entertain it per se, but rather by letting the emotion pass through me and releasing it. What also helps me, depending on the circumstances is stepping outside and moving my body, be it at the gym or going for a walk, or even just closing my eyes and taking a few deep breaths. It's important to be compassionate towards yourself, and to treat yourself with kindness and understanding. Recognise and validate your feelings and experiences without judgment, and just let them pass through you without holding onto them.

There are several methods available to reframe negative beliefs, process unresolved emotions, and integrate healing experiences. As such, it is important to note that unlearning is as crucial as learning. As we evolve and get closer to our true essence of who we're meant to be, or rather who we've always been, we must also recognise that this journey involves shedding outdated beliefs and emotional patterns, just like a butterfly. This process of unlearning allows us to release clinging to any emotions, particularly those rooted in past traumas and limiting thoughts. Given that we generally have a negative bias, it is essential to be specifically aware of how we might cling to these negative experiences, which no longer serve us. By intentionally addressing and letting go of these ingrained patterns, we make room for growth, adaptability, and a more authentic self. Embracing both the learning and unlearning processes enables us to achieve a balanced emotional state and move toward a more genuine and fulfilling existence.

Our formative experiences shape our beliefs and emotional responses, many of which are rooted in early childhood and become deeply ingrained over time, as we briefly touched on. To heal and grow, we must first identify these limiting beliefs such as feelings of unworthiness or fears that stem from past experiences. Recognising these beliefs involves introspection and confronting uncomfortable truths about ourselves. Once we've identified them, we need to reevaluate and challenge these assumptions, a process that may involve cognitive restructuring to replace distorted beliefs with more balanced perspectives.

Processing unresolved emotions is another key aspect of unlearning. This involves revisiting past traumas or disappointments and allowing ourselves to fully experience and express these emotions, which can be facilitated through therapeutic methods or expressive activities. As we work through these unresolved feelings, it's crucial to integrate new, positive experiences into our lives. This could mean forming new habits, building supportive relationships, or engaging in activities that affirm our worth and capabilities. These positive experiences help to build a new, healthier framework for understanding ourselves and interacting with the world.

Ultimately, the process of unlearning helps us align with our true essence - the person we were always meant to be, free from the constraints of past conditioning. Embracing our authentic self involves recognising and nurturing our innate strengths, desires, and values. This journey of unlearning is continuous: as we grow and evolve, new challenges may emerge, and old patterns might resurface. Maintaining a commitment to self-awareness, self-compassion, and ongoing reflection ensures that we stay aligned with our true essence and continue to integrate healing experiences effectively. In essence, unlearning outdated beliefs and emotional patterns is not just about letting go of the past but about actively creating space for a more authentic and fulfilling future.

At some point, I'd like to believe that we can break the mold of the generational burdens stemming from ineffective disciplinary methods, often rooted in fear, shame, guilt, or sheer ignorance; ineffective communication; emotional suppression, where vulnerability is seen as weakness; avoidance of conflict, leading to emotional distance; unmet emotional needs projected onto children; the glorification of struggle as a measure of worth; fear of change or failure; and the lack of accountability that keeps us stuck in cycles of blame and victimhood. True healing begins when we become conscious enough to respond rather than react. By consciously choosing more compassionate and constructive approaches, we can foster healthier relationships with our children, which I believe will set them up for a joyful, meaningful life ahead of them. Embracing positive discipline techniques, such as open communication, setting clear boundaries, and encouraging emotional expression I believe allows us to guide our children with understanding rather than fear. This shift not only empowers our children to develop resilience and self-esteem but also helps us create a nurturing environment where they can thrive. By letting go of outdated practices, we pave the way for a new legacy of supportive and loving parenting that prioritises growth and connection over control.

It is crucial for children to be allowed to develop as their own unique individuals from a young age. Teaching these fundamental principles in schools would be so very beneficial, as in a way, I believe it surpasses the importance of traditional academic learning in those crucial years where children may not be getting the skills and information needed for them to thrive in their family home. By deepening our self-awareness and practicing the skills that help us regulate our emotions, we learn to trust our inner voice and understand ourselves on a deeper level. This not only allows us to show up more authentically but also creates the foundation for children to thrive in all aspects of life - especially when it comes to their mental and emotional well-being. This early education in self-awareness and emotional intelligence equips them with essential tools for navigating life's complexities and fostering personal growth. Here I am not promoting to solve all your kids problems, but rather to teach them the tools necessary for them to do so for themselves, in a manner that is not destructive to them or others.

There are several methods available to help children reframe negative beliefs, by processing their emotions, and developing healthy coping strategies. For children, learning the process of unlearning is crucial, even though their experiences may not be as accumulated or deeply entrenched as those of adults. As they grow, it is essential for them to understand that letting go of unhelpful thoughts and emotions can foster emotional resilience. Children, while not having the same depth of past traumas or emotional patterns as adults, can still develop negative biases and cling to fears or misconceptions. By teaching them how to recognise and address these early negative patterns, we can help them build a foundation for healthier emotional regulation and adaptability, which I strongly believe is connected to the way they experience life. This process supports their ability to navigate challenges with a balanced perspective and cultivates a positive and authentic sense of self, preparing them for more fulfilling interactions and experiences as they continue to grow.

For instance, emotions like sadness, anger, or frustration, often labelled as negative, serve important purposes. They can signal unmet needs, prompt reflection, or motivate change. Embracing these emotions rather than dismissing or suppressing them can foster emotional resilience and personal growth. Instead of viewing emotions through a binary lens, it may be more beneficial to understand that all emotions have value and contribute to our overall well-being. Encouraging children to accept and explore their full range of feelings by recognising that both "negative" and "positive" emotions are part of the human experience can empower them to process their emotions more healthily and constructively.

It all starts though by us modelling what all of the above looks like.

5 SURRENDER TO THE FLOW OF LIFE

I find that the harder I push at something, anything really, the more resistance I encounter, almost as if the universe is insisting on teaching me the value of surrender and the value of patience. I see this unfold every time I try to push too hard at something which is ultimately out of my control – this sort of behaviour on my part shifts my energy and feelings to a place of desperation, frustration, tension or anxiety, depending on the specific scenario. Surrendering doesn't mean giving up, but rather, it's about being open to possibilities we might miss while fixating on a specific outcome, such as for example me expecting my daughter to understand concepts that I am still navigating myself. This impatience can create pressure and resistance, making it harder for her to engage. A key lesson I recently tried to share with her was that no one can make her feel a particular way and that she is responsible for her reactions to the world around her.

When we communicate generally speaking, but especially with children, they often sense the energy behind our words rather than the words themselves. Words carry a specific frequency, and their impact goes beyond just their surface meaning. When we communicate forcefully for example, as I sometimes do with my daughters before realizing what I am doing, and I am trying to persuade her to adopt my point of view, it can come across as overbearing and controlling. This forcefulness can create resistance rather than openness, making the other person feel pressured and invalidated, which results in a counterproductive reaction. For instance, when we aim to teach a lesson to our children but approach it with impatience or intensity, the energy behind our words often overshadows the intended message. People, especially children, are incredibly perceptive and can sense when our words lack authenticity or when they come from a place of forcefulness. This disconnect can lead to mistrust or confusion, causing them to shut down or react defensively instead of absorbing the lesson. The emotional resonance behind our words plays a crucial role in how our message is received. Genuine expression, aligned with our true feelings, creates a stronger connection and fosters a more meaningful interaction. A more effective approach would be to invite discussion and share insights in a way that encourages exploration rather than imposition and if you don't have the time to deep dive into such a discussion, withhold such until a better time to do so presents itself. By creating a space for open conversation, we allow others to feel valued and that makes them more willing to engage with the ideas being presented. This way, the lesson can be received more organically, leading to deeper understanding and connection. It's the combination of words and the underlying energy that truly communicates our intentions. Children have an innate ability to pick up on our emotions and they react accordingly, even if they don't fully understand why. Same applies for adult interactions.

As my awareness continues to grow, I find myself increasingly attuned to my internal beliefs and thoughts, which often dictate how I perceive the world around me, the way I communicate and act. It has become evident that when I try to force situations, the outcomes rarely align with my desires, no matter how intensely I push or how quickly I wish for things to unfold. This relentless striving often leaves me feeling anxious and stressed, and at times, wanting to scream in frustration, questioning, "Can I just get a break?". In reflecting on this thought, I now recognise that it embodies a victim mindset, taking the easy route of diverting my attention from taking accountability for my own feelings and the thought patterns that led me there. Instead of acknowledging my power to shape my reactions and perceptions, I seek an escape from the very emotions I need to confront. This realisation is groundbreaking as I believe it applies to all of us - it shows me that my experiences aren't dictated by external circumstances. In retrospect, I have tested this principle from every conceivable angle, often operating on autopilot, trying to control specific outcomes and striving for what I think should happen. Each time, I encounter the same unyielding resistance, reinforcing the lesson that true progress comes from letting go rather than pushing harder. By taking ownership of my journey and embracing this understanding, I can cultivate a sense of ease and trust in the process, shifting my focus from control to acceptance and empowering my growth.

As the meticulous person that I am, I've noticed a pattern: the moment I relax my mental grip by stilling the mind and loosen the internal barriers caused by limited belief systems of the past, that's when things start to flow, almost effortlessly and materialise in unexpected ways, often even better than initially envisioned. In essence, I am convinced that through our thought patterns and belief systems which are very much intricately linked, we cause ourselves a tremendous amount of misery and suffering – this of course is linked to the concept of knowing yourself.

When I refer to "mental grip," I'm talking about the intense focus and effort we exert when we try to control every aspect of a situation, which of course is ridiculous as we have no control over anything other than ourselves and more particularly how we react to life's unknowns. This grip often involves an almost obsessive preoccupation with outcomes, leading to stress and a sense of constant pressure. On a psychological level, it can manifest as an overactive prefrontal cortex, which is responsible for decision-making and managing potential threats. This area of the brain can generate excessive doubt and anxiety when we try to force things to happen according to our plan, creating a cycle of tension and resistance. At the same time while freeing yourself from overthinking can foster spontaneity and creativity, it's equally important to recognise that acting solely on impulse can lead to decisions that don't align with your values or long-term goals. This brings us back to the idea of avoiding acting on impulse, emphasising the need for reflection before making choices and acting upon them.

Finding that sweet spot between embracing flexibility and exercising discernment allows you to navigate your decisions more effectively. Letting go of mental rigidity opens up new possibilities, but taking a moment to assess your impulses ensures that any spontaneous actions resonate with your vision. By cultivating awareness and reflecting on your desires in the context of your goals, you can make choices that feel both authentic and intentional. Striking this balance ultimately leads to a more fulfilling journey, where you can enjoy the present while remaining grounded in your aspirations and personal growth.

When I refer to "internal barriers," on the other hand, I refer to the psychological blocks and self-imposed limitations that prevent us from moving forward. These barriers might include ingrained beliefs about what is possible and what isn't, fears of failure or inadequacy, and negative self-talk that undermines our confidence. Internally, these barriers often result from past experiences and conditioning, which shape our perceptions and reactions. They create a mental environment where growth and progress are stifled by self-doubt and rigidity.

When I let go of this mental grip and begin to dismantle these internal barriers, which sometimes takes a moment to reflect and register, a shift occurs. By easing the pressure and relaxing the need to control every detail, including people and events in my everyday life, I open myself up to the natural flow of life, events and attract more of that which I put out there. This change allows things to unfold more smoothly and brings about unexpected results, but the best one of them all, inner peace. Surrendering, or letting go, is not just an abstract concept but a practical approach to overcoming obstacles that would ordinarily throw us off, possibly make us loose composure and torture us until we are ready to let go. It helps in maintaining a sense of peace and joy in the present moment, allowing us to navigate challenges with greater ease and clarity. This takes practice and every now and then you will slip up, just as I do, but it's what you do that counts when you do slip up – stay accountable, rectify where necessary, yet avoid judgment and do better next time.

Surrendering, in this context, is intricately connected to the practice of being fully present in the moment. It's about immersing ourselves in the here and now, rather than being consumed by past regrets or future anxieties. This presence demands that we shift our focus away from what has already happened or what might happen, and instead, engage deeply with our current experience, which is the only thing that exists right now. By concentrating on the present, we allow ourselves to experience life as it unfolds naturally, without the added layers of worry or anticipation that often cloud our judgment and actions.

Being present in the moment requires a significant leap of faith - trusting that life will unfold in its own time and often in ways that are beyond our immediate understanding or control. It means accepting that outcomes might not align with our specific plans or expectations but are likely to emerge in ways that are just as valuable, if not more so. This trust can be particularly challenging for those of us who are inclined to seek control and predictability. We often strive to manage every detail and anticipate every possible outcome, believing that this control will lead to success or prevent failure, when it seldomly does.

Ironically, it turns out that the most effective way to achieve a sense of control over our lives is through the practice of surrender. When I began to let go of my rigid need for control and embraced the concept of surrender, I discovered that life became less of a struggle and more of a fluid journey. Surrendering doesn't mean giving up or resigning ourselves to passivity, but rather, it means releasing the tight grip on how things should unfold and allowing ourselves to flow with the natural rhythms of life, remaining flexible and responsive. This shift not only alleviates stress but also opens up space for greater enjoyment, adaptability and of course, outcomes too.

By surrendering, we paradoxically gain a more profound sense of control - not over specific outcomes, but over our own responses and attitudes. It's almost comical how we get so hung up on some things we have no control over, such as the weather for example, frustrated when it doesn't match the vision in our minds - as if we have any control over it. But isn't that just a reflection of how we move through life? Clinging to expectations, resisting what is, instead of learning to adapt. In the end, it's never the rain that ruins our day, but our resistance to it. We need to learn to navigate life with a sense of ease and confidence, accepting that while we may not control every variable, we can control how we engage with and respond to the unfolding process. This approach fosters a more harmonious and fulfilling experience, where control is less about dominating circumstances and more about aligning with the natural flow of our journey. There's often an expectation that someone else will step in - someone to do the work for you, cook for you, clean for you, or handle the difficult tasks. But what if, instead, you took full ownership of your life? What if you carried yourself with enough self-respect, dignity, and purpose to take responsibility for your own path? There's something profoundly empowering about doing things for yourself - not out of obligation, but out of a deep sense of personal integrity. When you stop waiting for someone else to make things happen for you and you step into your own power, you'll be amazed at what unfolds.

It's important to understand that surrendering doesn't mean letting go of ambition or vision. It simply means releasing the need to control every detail of the process. It's about taking action - whether it's starting a task, project, or workout - without waiting to feel "ready" or be in the "right" mindset. Because if we wait for the right mindset to begin, we'll end up doing very little and remain stagnant. The shift happens whilst you're in motion, not before it. Surrendering on the other hand is about focusing on our overarching goals and intentions while allowing the path to unfold organically. This approach enables us to align with the greater flow of life, which is always evolving and shifting. Through this alignment, we open ourselves to possibilities that might not fit within our initial plans but are nonetheless valuable, and perhaps even more valuable than we can acknowledge at first.

In practice, I've discovered that forcing situations rarely yields positive outcomes. If a situation doesn't bring a sense of ease, certainty, and clarity, it often signals the need to step back and reassess. This doesn't mean abandoning our efforts or giving up on our goals, but it's about recognising when to pause and listen to our inner guidance, and perhaps adjust if needed. By tuning into our intuition and allowing ourselves to adapt, we make decisions that are more closely aligned with our true purpose and greater vision. As in, we have to remain flexible.

Surrendering thus becomes a dynamic process of balance, where we actively pursue our goals while remaining open to the natural flow of change and growth. It's about engaging deeply with our intentions without rigidly dictating every step of the journey. This approach fosters a sense of harmony and adaptability, making our pursuit of success more fluid and aligned with the evolving nature of our lives.

Intuition, normally described as a form of rapid, unconscious processing based on accumulated experiences, allows us to make decisions beyond the scope of our immediate knowledge, however, the level of intuition that I am referring to here, can guide us beyond the constraints of our immediate experiences by drawing from deeper, more universal sources of guidance. This form of knowing can provide insights that transcend our conscious understanding, drawing from a collective wisdom or higher self that connects us to broader truths.

In the early stages of developing your intuition, trusting this inner guidance can be challenging, as it feels like there's just so much at stake. However, as you cultivate this skill, through practice, you will begin to access insights that are informed not just by your personal experiences but by a more expansive, universal perspective. This higher self, or intuitive wisdom, operates on a level that integrates past experiences with a broader, more holistic understanding of your path and purpose.

Neuroscience supports this process through the concept of neuroplasticity - the brain's remarkable ability to reorganise itself by forming new neural connections throughout life. As you refine and learn to trust your inner knowing, you essentially rewire your brain to better recognise and respond to deeper insights. This alignment with your higher self allows you to make choices that are more congruent with your true journey and purpose, leading to outcomes that are both fulfilling and effective.

In my professional life as a lawyer, considering various "what if" scenarios is crucial to serving my clients' interests effectively. This thorough examination of potential outcomes or risk factors is an essential part of the legal process, where anticipation and preparedness are key. However, in my personal life, I aim to transcend the "what if" mindset. Here, focusing too much on hypothetical scenarios can detract from enjoying the present and can create unnecessary anxiety, although by all means – do your research and only then make an informed decision which also considers your internal sensory system or inner knowing .

Balancing these aspects requires acknowledging the inherent contradiction: the need to explore potential outcomes in a professional context while striving to let go of such concerns in personal matters. By embracing the process of personal growth and trusting in my alignment with my higher self, I can navigate life's challenges with clarity and presence, rather than being consumed by speculative anxieties. This mindset allows me to experience joy and balance in my personal life while maintaining sharp analysis and strategic thinking in my professional life. Though both are part of the same life, each requires a different approach. Sometimes, growth requires us to distinguish between the different parts of ourselves - the version that shows up in our career, in our relationships, in solitude, or in moments of creativity. By honoring each aspect with intention, I can move between these spaces with awareness, preventing the stress of one from bleeding into another. This is where true inner freedom begins.

Understanding the theory of surrender is one thing, but applying it in your daily life can present its own set of challenges. You might wonder, "How do I know I'm on the right path, so I can surrender?" and "How long does it take to rewire my brain and adopt new, beneficial habits?" Neuroscience, particularly the concept of neuroplasticity, offers insights into these questions. Neuroplasticity, which is the brain's ability to reorganise itself by forming new neural connections, supports the idea that significant personal change is achievable, however, you are the only one that can make it happen and that requires more than just wanting to do so, it requires proactive and consistent effort in the form of action.

To determine if you're on the right path, look for signs of internal resonance and alignment with your values. Decisions that align with your true self often bring a sense of inner peace or excitement, rather than anxiety. Regular reflection and feedback on your progress, as well as trusting your inner knowing, can also guide you. If your choices feel right and are moving you closer to your long-term goals, you are likely on the right track.

When it comes to rewiring your brain and adopting new habits, the process requires consistent practice over time - often weeks to months, and now and then, in a moment of weakness you can fall back into old habits. However, the shift itself can happen in an instant, the moment you make a conscious decision to stop looking back and commit to moving forward. Consistency, engagement, and a supportive environment are key to reinforcing these new patterns. The more motivated and intentional you are, the faster your brain adapts. But sustaining that momentum requires more than just willpower - it's about keeping your mindset in check and prioritising self-care, fitness, quality sleep, and overall well-being. It's a holistic process - the whole shebang. Additionally, mindfulness and self-reflection help maintain awareness of your progress and allow for adjustments as needed.

In essence, integrating the theory of surrender into your life requires a blend of patience, persistence, and self-compassion. By focusing on aligning with your true path and embracing the process of change, you can navigate personal growth more effectively. Trust that challenges will be manageable as they arise, rather than getting stuck in "what if" scenarios or beating yourself up when you don't respond as you would have wanted to after reflection. This allows you to stay present and enjoy the journey while achieving more meaningful outcomes. Most importantly, don't let a moment of deviation or a dip in energy undo all your hard work. When you slip up or fall off track, resist the urge to spiral into self-criticism. Simply adjust, realign, and keep moving forward. Allow yourself to just be, knowing you are fully capable of handling whatever comes your way - even if that means redirecting your path every now and then.

Throughout my own journey, I have encountered a great deal of resistance, which is predominantly my own doing, which can be discouraging and exhausting. At times, I've felt like giving up, questioning why achieving anything seemed to require so much effort and why was such linked to so much struggle. I've been taught that nothing worth having comes easy, a belief that has been deeply ingrained in me. This sort of belief is often passed down through generations, and this has made resistance seem almost necessary for success.

However, in recent years, I've discovered that life and everything we do need not be so fraught with resistance. By focusing on understanding ourselves and embracing our true nature by stilling the mind and its constant chatter, we can uncover inner strengths, vision and purpose like we never knew we had, which in turn can lead us to living joyfully with a sense of fulfilment, cultivate healthy relationships and a deep sense of wholeness. Surrendering to the unknown and trusting my inner wisdom - whether it's intuition, gut feeling, or whatever other term you wish to give it, has proven transformative for me. True inner wisdom feels calm, certain and even exciting, unlike the doubts and anxieties often stirred by the prefrontal cortex. Learning to distinguish between the two has helped me navigate life's challenges with greater clarity and trust.

Ultimately, change is the only constant in life. Everything else calls for trust and surrender. When we embrace surrender, life begins to align and unfold effortlessly. I believe that spiritual evolution is inevitable, and for those who resist it, life's challenges may act as catalysts. While such lessons may not be entirely avoidable, perhaps their edges can be softened if we are a little more proactive. By consciously shaping our lives and destinies, we honour our innate potential to evolve and thrive.

6 ACCEPTANCE OF ALL AS IT IS

I am still practicing acceptance of all things, beings, and parts of life, for only then can we experience the greatest gift of all - internal peace, joy, and appreciation for all that we have and all that we are at this very moment. This is not with the idea of fooling ourselves into thinking that everything is perfect, morally, ethically, or otherwise, but rather about finding peace and gratitude in the present moment, whatever that may look like. A good starting point would be acceptance of yourself, just the way you are today - not necessarily who you were in the past, but strictly who you are in this moment, and the power you have to redirect, reinvent, or otherwise upgrade yourself in any way you choose. We often compare ourselves not only to others but also to younger versions of ourselves: perhaps when we were fitter, healthier, or more vibrantand feel dissatisfied with where we are now. This can be a result of aging or neglecting certain aspects of our well-being, making it essential to nurture ourselves as we transition through life to maintain longevity, health, and overall vitality. I feel we don't give ourselves enough grace and patience, and we fail to put enough distance between the old versions of ourselves and the person we are today. We often find ourselves mercilessly revisiting moments of pain and suffering, allowing these experiences to replay in our minds. Instead of accepting things as they are, we tend to dwell on the hurt, creating an ongoing cycle that is hard to break. This tendency to reexperience our past can prevent us from moving forward, embracing the present, and truly living, keeping us trapped in a constant state of pain and suffering.

Acceptance is a crucial step in this process. It involves acknowledging feelings without allowing them to define us and letting them go. While we cannot change the past, we do have the power to shape our future through utilising the power of the present moment, releasing past experiences when they surface and remaining present. If we truly desire change, we must take actionable steps toward it, today, and every day thereafter. This is a way of life, not a bootcamp, although with each day you will notice a shift in your way of being should you fully apply yourself and want it strongly enough.

This perspective invites us to focus not on the difficulties we are experiencing themselves, but on the opportunities for growth and healing that lie in the present moment. It encourages reflection on what we can learn from our experiences and how we can use those lessons to foster positive change. Ultimately, accepting our past by releasing bottled up emotions enables us to channel our energy into constructive actions, freeing us from the weight of regret, pain and suffering and opening the door to new possibilities. In embracing this mindset, we allow ourselves to heal and grow, transforming suffering into strength and resilience.

For as long as we do our best, with what we have, even a little bit at a time then inevitably we will be presented with opportunities of growth and evolvement, for ultimately that's what we are all here to do, should this be something you want to do of course. Let's accept where we are today and also accept that we are constantly changing, evolving and growing and today is most likely a place we dreamt we'd be some time back, at least in some aspects of our lives. Let's recognise our achievements and all the progress made to date and enjoy it fully, wholeheartedly in this present moment, instead of rushing off to the next thing or focusing on the one thing that isn't going according to our liking. I'd also like to add a little blurb for those that may have done something wrong in their past that they are not proud of, those that have hurt people, be it intentionally or not – all of this applies to you too! You have just been unable to control yourself and your primitive urges (we all have those-it does not mean we should act upon them) when your emotional wastebasket spillover happened and triggered your bottled up pain – this is what maybe made you feel strong, in control and alive and it is not too late to shift those ways, clear your own inner wastebasket by letting it go next time it tries to surface and live a dignified, peaceful and joyful life forward.

The glimpses of successfully accomplishing this task are so worthwhile and rewarding and an indicator of great things coming your way, for no matter how small or big, you have a different sense of appreciation for everything around you. Allow to be thrilled every step of the way by joyfully and gracefully embracing the human range of emotions, the vast variety of experiences and encounters and may each one serve, metaphorically speaking, as just another tool in your toolbox of life. There is nothing you cannot handle and come back from, no matter how difficult, although you may be forever changed in the way you perceive the world. Life presents us with challenges that can feel overwhelming, yet within each struggle lies the potential for resilience and acceptance. When we encounter hardship, we often discover strengths we didn't know we had, learning to embrace our emotions and the reality of our situations rather than resisting them.

Acceptance is a powerful force in the healing process. It encourages us to acknowledge our experiences without judgment, creating the space to process our pain and letting it go. By simply observing our pain without reacting, we allow it to dissipate just like clouds drafting and transforming in the sky. Visualising this process of imagining a cloud dissolving and changing can bring clarity and peace, so this may serve as a great tool the next time you feel triggered or feel a shift in your energy. This doesn't mean we condone what has happened or that we aren't affected by it, but rather, it empowers us to recognise that we have the capacity to rise from our difficulties and take charge of what we can control, the way we react and perceive a situation. When we accept our circumstances, we free ourselves from the burden of denial and resistance, enabling us to see the lessons that adversity can teach.

As we navigate our challenges, we may find that our perceptions of the world shift significantly. We may become more compassionate, recognising the struggles of others as reflections of our own. Our values might realign, prompting us to seek deeper connections and to appreciate the beauty in life's fleeting moments. Acceptance can foster a greater sense of gratitude, urging us to cherish what we have rather than dwelling on what we've lost or what we wish we had.

This transformation is not about returning to who we were before but embracing the new layers of ourselves that have emerged from our experiences. As we learn to accept both the light and the dark aspects of our journey, we become more resilient and open to the possibilities that lie ahead. Ultimately, while challenges may leave their mark, they also offer opportunities for profound growth, teaching us that acceptance is not just a way to cope but a pathway to deeper understanding and a richer, more authentic life.

When we embrace the parts of us that we're not necessarily proud of, and possibly even ashamed of, we release ourselves of the very thing that burdens our soul and weighs heavy on our conscious. We basically make a conscious choice that we will not allow events, people or circumstances define who we are and how we choose to live our life, for as long as we do so in a dignified manner and do not cause harm to others. The past can't be undone, fixed or otherwise manipulated and through it all, there would have been a deeply embedded lesson, which should not be overlooked, and that would inevitably help you free yourself from the shackles you placed on yourself, weighing yourself down. We are not victims and we are the creators of our own destiny - everything passes unless attention is given to it. The Serenity Prayer carries a lot of wisdom and is widely embraced in recovery communities, but what if we approached life with this mindset from the start, before turning to unhealthy coping mechanisms or forms of escapism? Its essence can be reframed in a universally inclusive way, resonating with both believers and non-believers alike: "May I find the serenity to accept the things I cannot change, the willpower to change the things I can, and the wisdom to discern the difference.". This perspective fosters balance, clarity, and a sense of contentment in navigating life's challenges.

Everything we give our attention to, starting from having a thought, which is very often something our mind just generates without your input per se based on your internal record system, observations and beliefs, multiplies and expands, often out of proportion. Our minds are incredibly influential, and the thoughts we nurture can significantly shape our belief systems, and in turn, our reality, especially if we don't take the reins and guide the mind in the desired direction. When we focus on a particular idea, emotion or event, we inadvertently feed it with energy, allowing it to grow and evolve. Being mindful of where we direct our attention becomes crucial in maintaining a balanced perspective. Understanding the origin of our thoughts is essential in discerning their validity and relevance. Thoughts can arise from various sources, and recognising their roots can help us navigate our mental landscape more effectively. First, some thoughts may emerge from our higher self, that inner voice that aligns with our core values, intuition, and authentic desires. This part of us often promotes self-acceptance, love, and growth, encouraging us to pursue goals that resonate with our true selves. When we tune into this voice and headspace, our thoughts can be empowering and constructive, guiding us toward fulfilling paths. These thoughts are typically marked by clarity, a sense of knowing, and a feeling of alignment with our values. On the other hand, many thoughts can be the byproducts of external influences or simply mind-generated. Society, cultural norms, family expectations, and media narratives all contribute to the shaping of our beliefs and perceptions, if we allow them to and when we are young we tend to follow what we are told or demonstrated. Often, we internalise messages from our surroundings without questioning their validity. For example, societal standards of success or beauty can lead to negative self-talk and feelings of inadequacy. Recognising when our thoughts are rooted in external validation rather than our authentic selves is vital in preventing unnecessary stress and anxiety. Additionally, our mind's tendency to overthink can generate a barrage of thoughts that may not accurately reflect reality. This mental habit can stem from anxiety, a desire for control, or a fear of the unknown. When we're caught in this cycle, our minds may magnify problems, conjuring scenarios that amplify our worries. This is often a defense mechanism, an attempt to prepare for potential outcomes, but it can lead us to spiral into negativity. It's crucial to remember that not every thought we have is a reflection of the truth.

The saying "don't believe everything you think" serves as a powerful reminder of this. Thoughts are just that - thoughts. They are not facts. By cultivating mindfulness, we can create a space between our thoughts and our reactions, allowing us to question their validity before accepting them as truth. This practice empowers us to choose where we focus our attention and how we respond to our internal narratives.

In this way, mindfulness becomes a tool for discernment. By reflecting on the origins of our thoughts, we can assess whether they stem from our higher self, external influences, or the anxieties of overthinking. This awareness allows us to let go of thoughts that don't serve us, replacing them with those that foster growth, resilience, and authenticity. Ultimately, the journey toward a balanced perspective begins with understanding and questioning the thoughts we choose to engage with and to what extent, enabling us to live more intentionally and harmoniously.

The more grateful we are for example, the more we have to be grateful for. We are capable of so much more than we will ever be fully able to understand or express -sometimes it's just a feeling, an indescribable sensation that transcends words and logic. Human potential is vast and multi-layered, often extending beyond the confines of our conscious understanding. Within each of us lies a reservoir of strength, creativity, and resilience that can surface in unexpected ways.

These feelings, which often elude precise description, are powerful indicators of our inner potential. They can manifest as a rush of inspiration, a surge of motivation, or even a profound sense of connectedness to something greater than ourselves. In these moments, we may find ourselves touched by an ineffable force that propels us to act, create, or connect deeply with others. This sense of urgency or drive can be challenging to articulate, yet it often serves as a catalyst for personal growth and transformation.

Consider the creative process that artists, writers, and musicians frequently draw from this well of indescribable feeling, channelling emotions and experiences into their work. These creations resonate with others precisely because they capture the essence of feelings that are often difficult to put into words. The beauty of art lies in its ability to convey the inexpressible, allowing us to connect on a deeper level, often without fully understanding why.

Moreover, our potential is also shaped by our experiences and the lessons we learn throughout life. Many of our capabilities are not immediately apparent: they unfold gradually as we navigate challenges, embrace opportunities, and push beyond our perceived limits. It is in these moments of struggle and triumph that we discover aspects of ourselves we never knew existed. Sometimes, the realisation of our capabilities arrives as a fleeting feeling - an instinct or intuition that urges us to step outside our comfort zones.

The complexities of our emotions further illustrate this point. We can experience joy, sorrow, love, and fear simultaneously, often feeling them in ways that defy explanation. These intertwined emotions can guide our decisions and influence our paths, even when we struggle to articulate them. This depth of feeling enriches our human experience, reminding us that understanding ourselves is an ongoing journey rather than a finite destination.

Ultimately, acknowledging that we possess untapped potential encourages us to embrace the unknown and the indescribable. It invites us to be open to new experiences, to trust our inner wisdom and ourselves, and to explore the depths of our creativity, resilience and the strength of our willpower. While we may never fully grasp the entirety of our capabilities, allowing ourselves to feel and engage with those indescribable sensations can lead to profound insights and growth, revealing the extraordinary within the mundane as we experience in our everyday lives.

We all embark on a personal journey to discover our true selves from the very day we are born, navigating the influences of external elements such as that of family, education, and societal expectations along the way. As we navigate life, challenges such as financial pressures, family responsibilities, illness, and emotional suffering often lead us to question our existence. We may find ourselves asking, "Is this all there is to life?", "Who am I beyond the obvious?" or even "What's the purpose of life?" While the answers differ for each individual, the act of questioning itself signals an awakening, a readiness to seek deeper truth. What sparks this inquiry matters less than the fact that it happens at all.

In my life, I have had several "teachers" and none of them were actually teachers, but I would say the biggest awakening in my personal life started with my daughters for me. Their ability to mirror what I have not dealt with, be it in my childhood or adulthood, often through resistance and push-back, has prompted me to confront unresolved emotions and past experiences I had not dealt with and had buried deep within, way out of sight, without even realising that those are all contributing factors to the way I thought, acted and otherwise moved through life. As I observe their unfiltered expressions of joy, frustration, and curiosity, I begin to recognise how much I have held back - how many parts of myself I had hidden away out of fear, shame and I guess to some extent, self-preservation.

Growing up, I was often surrounded by the sounds of my parents arguing, their bickering filling the air with tension and unease. Conflict was ever-present, yet never constructive, leaving me both intolerant of it and unequipped to handle it - despite the inevitability of disagreement in life. Looking back, I always had a strong sense of what was right for me (and others) and what needed to be said or done, but I lacked the skills to express it in a way that would be well-received. Though I had the "chutzpah" as my sister in law would say, my naivety and deeply trusting nature left me vulnerable to manipulation, as I assumed others approached life with the same sincerity I did. And time and again, I learned the hard way that they didn't. My struggle was not just about communication; it stemmed from not fully knowing my own strength, the value I brought, or the power of my intuition. With time, I've honed the ability to discern what people say versus what they truly mean, to trust my instincts, and to navigate interactions with clarity - no longer easily swayed, but firmly anchored in who I am.

My journey toward acceptance began unexpectedly through learning to resolve conflict - accepting its inevitability in life rather than avoiding it out of fear. By accepting conflict as a natural part of human interaction, I found the freedom to develop the very skills I needed to navigate it effectively. Even the slightest disagreement on a personal level once sent me spiraling into discomfort and anxiety, making me avoid confrontation at all costs. But life has a way of forcing growth, and witnessing the dishonesty and lack of morality in business was a harsh wake-up call for me - revealing not only how far people would go for a buck but also how unequipped I was to navigate it. I despised the chaos so much that I became determined to master the art of reading the room and handling conflict efficiently. When I eventually pursued law, I felt I had found my calling. I threw myself into situations that required conflict resolution, quickly learning that the sooner you address an issue, the better - but only if you approach it with a still mind, free from the grip of heightened emotion. Reacting from a place of unchecked emotion is dangerous: more often than not, it's just the ego riding high waves, distorting clarity. By nature, I am a settler - I don't believe in fighting for the sake of it. But if the need arises, I can, and I will. True conflict resolution is an art form - one that demands not only knowledge and practice but also deep self-awareness, an understanding of human nature, and the discipline to manage your own emotions, biases, and perspectives. Having a strong intuition further sharpens this skill, offering an invaluable guide in reading people and situations - cutting through the noise, revealing unspoken truths, and allowing for a response that is both precise and effective.

A pivotal aspect of conflict resolution is strong communication skills. I've come to realise that addressing conflicts with calmness and precision, rather than reacting from fear or defensiveness, can completely shift the outcome. Approaching disagreements with clarity and intention fosters honest dialogue and understanding, preventing unnecessary escalation. As lawyers, we can easily tip the scales in either direction, and I'm convinced that a deliberate choice goes into shaping the desired result. That said, some individuals thrive on conflict and negativity and, to put it politely, can be entirely unreasonable. It's crucial to recognise when communication alone isn't enough - it must be reinforced with decisive action. Staying true to yourself and upholding your core values is essential, and knowing when to step back is just as important as knowing when to engage. Disengaging from toxic or unproductive discussions can be a powerful act of self-respect. In some cases, seeking professional intervention - such as a mediator or therapist - can provide the necessary structure to navigate difficult situations. These neutral third parties offer valuable tools and strategies, helping you assert yourself effectively while maintaining consideration for the other person. Whether in personal or professional settings, external guidance can facilitate healthier communication, offer a more balanced perspective, and help mend strained relationships when direct dialogue alone isn't yielding progress.

Ultimately, it's about finding an approach that feels right for you while staying true to yourself. If a situation is salvageable, allow the other person the opportunity to explain or make amends - but if someone calls for a "truce" while their actions contradict their words, shut that door, because their intentions are clear. This might mean stepping away from a conversation when emotions are running high (with a polite excuse), seeking guidance, or exploring alternative resolutions. The key is to prioritise your well-being and ensure that your actions align with your core values. Don't hesitate to voice them - honest, open communication is far more powerful than living in the shadows of assumption, hearsay, or frustration. At the same time, be mindful that not everyone's intentions are pure, no matter how convincing they may seem. This is where tuning into your intuition becomes invaluable. Some people are simply proficient at presenting themselves well, but authenticity always reveals itself in time. The truth has a way of surfacing, and when it does, you'll be grateful you stayed grounded rather than getting caught up in illusions. Let it unfold as it will - your peace is worth more than the energy wasted on pretense.

My own journey has not been easy either: it has often felt like a battle to strip away those layers of protection and let go of the burdens that no longer serve me. Each step forward requires me to confront past experiences and emotions, and the resistance I feel reflects the internal struggle of releasing what I thought was safe. Yet, in acknowledging this discomfort, I create space for healing and growth. Embracing this journey has taught me the importance of vulnerability, reminding me that true strength lies in facing our past and releasing any emotional blockages, while forging a new path. This process can feel like you are going backwards, until one day, it doesn't.

The journey of personal growth and self-liberation is often illuminated by the guidance and support of others, who help us uncover the goodness within ourselves and inspire us to evolve. In every life, there are moments of connection and insight that spark transformation, reminding us of the innate potential we all carry, waiting to be recognised and nurtured.

True liberation begins with acknowledging the goodness already present in our lives and embracing the opportunities or help extended to us to grow. Whether it comes from a mentor, a friend, or a supportive presence, such guidance holds the power to lead us toward self-discovery and freedom from our inner tyrant - the critical voice that limits us and that has stored all sorts of things which were supposed to be released. We were never designed to cling to emotions or experiences indefinitely but to move through them: to feel, learn, and grow from them, then let them go with confidence. By releasing what no longer serves us, we create space to live fully, apply what we've learned, and navigate life with clarity and self-assurance.

Along my own path, I've been deeply enriched by the wisdom, compassion, and encouragement of remarkable and completely ordinary individuals. Their influence has not only helped me navigate challenges but has also inspired me to recognise and embrace my inner strength. These connections have illuminated parts of myself that I might not have discovered otherwise, offering perspectives that shaped my journey profoundly.

Through such relationships, we transcend personal limitations and discover a clarity to view the world through a lens of abundance and possibility. By taking the leap, accepting challenges and welcoming the kindness extended to us we not only elevate our own lives but also cultivate meaningful connections that reinforce growth, kindness, and shared purpose.

This path underscores the extraordinary value of authentic relationships, reminding us that growth and liberation are deeply intertwined with recognising the goodness in ourselves and others. Embracing this truth allows us to move forward with courage, clarity, and a renewed sense of self.

What I am trying to say is that acceptance is not passive: it is an active, conscious choice to see things as they are, without resistance, denial or sugar-coating. It does not mean condoning what is harmful or settling for less, but rather recognising that true power lies in how we respond, so make sure you get really good at it. When we accept our past without resentment, our emotions without shame, and our challenges without fear, we reclaim our energy and step into clarity. Acceptance allows us to move forward with intention, free from the weight of expectations, our own or those imposed upon us. It is the bridge between struggle and peace, between limitation and possibility. When we fully embrace both our journey and the lessons within it, we find that life itself has always been guiding us toward exactly where we need to be.

The path ahead remains uniquely yours to walk, but when approached with acceptance, even the most challenging terrain becomes doable. In accepting all as it is, we paradoxically create the space for everything to transform into what it could be.

7 THERE IS ONLY ONE WAY TO EAT AN ELEPHANT: ONE BITE AT A TIME

Life is full of challenges, and while we can't always control what happens to us and around us, we can control how we react, both internally and externally, in that order. Embracing difficulties as opportunities for growth allows us to tackle them with confidence, no matter the magnitude. Each challenge we face is not only an opportunity to learn more about ourselves, but also enables us to develop our resilience. By approaching these kind of situations one at a time, methodically, we can break them down into manageable parts, reducing feelings of overwhelm and enabling us to focus on solutions rather than problems. There's really only one way to eat an elephant: one bite at a time and yes, figuratively speaking – not promoting the eating of any actual elephants.

In a way, it's just shifting from an outcome-based approach to a process-based approach. This means placing less emphasis on achieving a specific result and more on the journey itself - immersing yourself in the steps, learning from each experience, and refining your own ways and methods along the way. By focusing on the process, you cultivate patience, a sense of presence, and appreciation for each moment. The act of persevering through the process becomes its own reward, fostering peace and satisfaction even before the goal is achieved. This mindset reduces anxiety tied to outcomes and encourages a sustainable, balanced way of approaching challenges. Ultimately, enjoying the process allows you to find meaning and fulfilment regardless of the results, creating a state of harmony between effort and acceptance.

From the moment we are born, we are equipped with a remarkable set of tools such as: intuition, curiosity, and a natural capacity for self-preservation. These guide us through early challenges with innate wisdom. However, something profound shifts in us as we transition from childhood to adulthood. This complex journey, marked by social, emotional, and cognitive changes, often distances us from our authentic selves. As we grow, societal ideals, peer influence, and the schooling system often overshadow our natural instincts and intuition – we are now told how and what to think. Sometimes, we don't even get to think as someone just tells us exactly what to do. The education system, while providing valuable knowledge, fails in one critical way in my personal opinion: it suppresses individuality, discourages self-reflection, and neglects to nurture our inner wisdom and intuition. Instead of fostering personal growth and creativity, it promotes conformity, teaching us to prioritise external validation over trusting our inner voice. This disconnect can lead to catastrophic outcomes, as many never rediscover the tools they were born with and rewiring your brain, changing your habits and belief systems, although possible, is very hard work as an adult and requires so much more will power to do so than if it was just there from the get go. And when this wisdom isn't fostered at home either, the cycle of disconnection deepens. Could this be intentional? A system designed to cultivate a compliant workforce with a suppressed mentality, limiting self-thought and critical awareness or perhaps heavily outdated? Regardless of which one it is, the question remains: how many will push through these deeply embedded belief systems, challenge societal conditioning, and reconnect with their inner wisdom? It takes immense perseverance to unlearn imposed ideas and rediscover the self and it's not exactly pleasant in the beginning, well at least until you have that "aha" moment and get excited about it all as you take charge and step away from victimhood mentality – you are not a victim. Yet those who do often embark on a transformative path, finding freedom and authenticity in a world that often discourages both. To truly nurture individuality and self-awareness, we must rethink the spaces where growth occurs - schools, universities, homes, workspaces and communities. These environments in order to function more optimally would have to prioritise fostering creativity, play, critical thinking, and inner wisdom, empowering individuals to trust themselves and navigate life with clarity and confidence. Only then can we break the cycle and cultivate a future that values both personal fulfilment and collective progress.

As human beings, we have a deep desire for acceptance, and this longing can sometimes create a cycle where we prioritize external opinions over our own, diminishing our ability to think independently and disconnecting us from our higher self - our inner guidance, which some may also refer to as intuition. In a world filled with conflicting narratives and societal expectations, this struggle can be especially intense for those who feel they don't fit into the mainstream. When faced with uncertainty about identity, values, or belonging, it's easy to seek validation from the outside world, sometimes to the point of losing sight of self-acceptance. For some, this can lead to an internal battle - questioning who they are, what they stand for, and where they truly belong. And in the most painful moments, this struggle can turn into an external demand for acceptance when the deepest challenge is the acceptance of oneself. It's a difficult and often exhausting cycle, but one that can only be broken by turning inward with compassion, self-reflection, and a willingness to embrace one's own truth - independent of societal approval. True peace comes not from forcing the world to validate our existence but from recognising that we are already whole, just as we are.

Additionally, the overwhelming influx of information from media and social networks clouds our judgment, further detaching us from our true knowing's and desires. There are just an exorbitant number of distractions out there and how does one stay focused and true to themselves? There is also the aspect of pursuit of love and validation outside ourselves, which often stems from a fear of sorts or desire to feel "complete", leading to emotional dependency that fosters dissatisfaction when external sources fail to provide affirmation and of course they will, as true love, satisfaction and everything that you will ever need can only come from within. As we navigate heightened responsibilities and expectations, the pressure to achieve can divert our focus from self-exploration to meeting societal demands, causing us to neglect our innate capacity for self-reflection and personal growth. It's not all bad news though, this disconnection from our intuition and authentic selves can be countered through self-discovery and mindfulness practices, empowering us to reclaim our inner voice, seek validation from within, and foster healthier, more genuine relationships. Our bodies follow where our minds have already arrived - we are always steering in the direction of our dominant thoughts, whether we realise it or not. While the exact path may be unclear, every choice we make today shapes where we end up tomorrow. Growth, change, and even the unexpected all stem from the intentions we set, the actions we take, and the mindset we cultivate. The key is to become conscious of this power, to recognise that we are not merely passengers in our own lives but the ones steering the ship.

We need to be aware and intentional in everything that we do, including the intake of information. There is an overwhelming influx of information, much of which may be completely irrelevant to our day-to-day lives, yet it can leave us feeling disoriented, in a state of distress or otherwise paralyzed. Not to mention, it is scientifically proven that our brains have negative biases, which predispose us to focus on and store negative experiences more so than positive ones. This negativity bias can extend beyond personal experiences, leading us to dwell on negative events or narratives that don't directly relate to us, further amplifying feelings such as anxiety, fear and self-doubt. This can happen in so many ways, through the content intake via the various mediums or simply that inner chatter fuelled by insecurities or fears that already live there. Be mindful of it all and where it comes from and be sure not to entertain it in terms of taking the emotional burden on, for it can spiral out of control.

I am intentionally hopping on the topic a little bit but it is highly relevant and very important to bring awareness to it, as I find that critical life skills and emotional intelligence topics are often overlooked, creating a gap that makes it challenging to adapt successfully to the complexities of adult life. This oversight can leave individuals feeling ill-equipped to navigate emotional challenges, manage relationships, and develop a strong sense of self, ultimately setting many on a path toward a rigid way of being rather than fostering individual growth and creativity, whatever that may look like.

This sort of disconnect can hinder our ability to navigate challenges effectively, leading to feelings of inadequacy, failure or frustration. As a result, many individuals may struggle with emotional regulation, problem-solving, and interpersonal relationships, all of which are essential for personal and professional success. Without the tools to manage these challenges, it becomes increasingly difficult to cultivate resilience and an open and optimal mindset. To address this, it's crucial to incorporate emotional intelligence training and practical life skills into educational curricula, into our homes and even work spaces ensuring that individuals are equipped to face the demands of adulthood with confidence and adaptability. By bridging this gap, we can help foster a generation that is not only aware of their emotional landscapes but also adept at navigating the complexities of life with confidence, resilience and a growth-oriented perspective.

Alongside the journey or transition period from childhood into adulthood, we often adopt methods and strategies that aren't authentically ours and that don't genuinely reflect who we are, that are not beneficial to us or those around us. In the process, we may start comparing ourselves to others through a skewed perception, as we can never fully know or understand where others truly are in their lives – that's for them to figure out. This comparison will most certainly mislead us, causing us to lose sight of our individuality and the authenticity of our own path. We can also easily become ensnared in the expectations of others, reshaping ourselves to fit molds that society, workplaces, family, or peers create for us. This transformation can result in a pollution of our minds with endless distractions and noise, diverting us from our true selves. In this process, we are likely to lose sight of our innate intuition, allowing external pressures to dictate our choices and desires. As we strive to meet these external expectations, we can stray further from who we genuinely are, feeling increasingly disconnected from our authentic selves.

Focusing too much on potential pitfalls can rob us of the joy that exists in the present moment. When we constantly anticipate negative outcomes, danger, failure, betrayal etc we shift our mindset to one of fear and anxiety. This not only diminishes our enjoyment of life but can also create a self-fulfilling prophecy. By fixating on what could go wrong, we divert our energy away from appreciating the here and now, missing out on the beauty and potential of our current experiences, and in turn attracting the very thing we so hard tried to avoid. There is such a powerful connection between our thoughts, which create energy and our reality and if we consistently think negatively, we are likely to unknowingly attract similar experiences into our lives. Our mindset shapes our perceptions and actions, influencing the way we navigate challenges. By cultivating a positive outlook and believing in our ability to handle whatever comes our way, we set the stage for more constructive and fulfilling experiences.

Our minds can either anchor us in negativity or propel us toward growth: the choice is yours. While every choice comes with its own set of challenges, the key is to choose the kind of "challenge" you are willing to take on. For instance, being fit is hard - it requires discipline, consistent effort, and overcoming the temptation to give up or give it a "miss" for a lazy evening in front of the TV with a comforting snack. But being unhealthy is also hard - it comes with constant fatigue, negative self-talk, lack of confidence, discomfort, and potential health complications. Similarly, working to maintain strong relationships is hard – yes, it demands communication, vulnerability, time and constant adjustment. Yet, loneliness and disconnection bring their own kind of hard. The point is, life is full of difficulties, no matter what path you choose, so why not pick the type of challenges that aligns with your goals and values instead of going like a dead fish with the flow? Move through life with intention, with purpose and with a deep sense of self-respect. Choosing your challenges means taking ownership of your life, of your decisions, understanding that growth and fulfilment often come through consistent effort and persistence. It's about finding meaning in the challenges you embrace and recognising that the hard work you choose is an investment in a better version of yourself.

I've applied this incremental approach to every significant goal in my life. When completing my legal studies, I focused on mastering one subject at a time rather than becoming overwhelmed by the entirety of law school. While building my business, I concentrated on serving each client exceptionally well instead of fixating on ambitious growth targets. Even this book came together one paragraph, one chapter at a time - some days writing flowed easily, other days I managed just a few lines, but the consistent progress eventually created something meaningful. This method has repeatedly shown me that patience and persistence make seemingly impossible goals achievable.

The rapid advancement of technology adds another layer of complexity to modern life. For those not immersed in the field, keeping up with ever-evolving platforms, digital trends, and new innovations can feel overwhelming and mentally exhausting. The constant influx of information and notifications can be paralyzing, making it difficult to discern what truly matters. Your mobile phone or smart watch as much as beeps and you immediately divert your attention to it. Not to mention, the algorithms that power much of the content we consume are designed to feed us more of what we show interest in. While this can be helpful when our interests are positive and constructive, it becomes deeply problematic when our focus is on destructive or unhealthy patterns. These algorithms amplify what we engage with, creating a feedback loop that reinforces negativity or harmful behaviours. Over time, this can shape our perspectives, habits, and even our mental well-being, making it all the more crucial to be mindful of the content we consume and the digital environments we inhabit, as those can lead to segregation pushing us further away from community relatability amongst many other things. As everyone's interests are structured through a tunnel vision, it becomes increasingly difficult to connect with others and find shared ground, causing a profound sense of disconnection. To avoid this, it's essential to consciously diversify the information and perspectives we expose ourselves to and to be extra mindful of this insofar as the younger generations are concerned, as they are simply put, not equipped for any of it with considering their brain is still developing. Actively seek out content and viewpoints that challenge your current beliefs and broaden your understanding of the world. Limit reliance on algorithms by exploring offline activities, fostering face-to-face connections, and engaging with community-driven initiatives that promote inclusivity and collaboration. Practice digital mindfulness by curating your online environment - unfollow sources that fuel negativity, subscribe to platforms that encourage diverse ideas, and set boundaries around screen time. Most importantly, nurture real-world relationships by finding commonality in shared values and experiences, reminding yourself and others that community and connection thrive when we embrace a wider, more empathetic perspective.

Embracing change and reconnecting with our authentic selves is essential, especially as we navigate life's inevitable ups and downs. There will always be moments when everything seems to align perfectly, when creativity flows, relationships thrive, and life feels fulfilling and harmonious. These are the times that fuel our motivation and remind us of what it feels like to be in synchronicity with our goals and values. Yet, life is never a straight or predictable path. Challenges and setbacks will come, testing our resolve and pushing us to adapt. It's in these moments of struggle that we often learn the most about ourselves. The journey is about recognising that the highs and lows are equally important, each contributing to our growth and perspective. When faced with difficult times, approaching them with patience and the understanding that they, too, shall pass can provide a sense of peace and resilience. Ultimately, life is about embracing the process, knowing that both the joys and challenges shape our experience of life. Each stage of life presents its own set of challenges that prepare us for the next phase of growth. The difficulties we face today are often the stepping stones to the strength and wisdom we will need tomorrow. When faced with adversity, it becomes a test of how much we truly want to return to our path and continue pursuing our goals. In moments like these, it's crucial to lean on the tools we've cultivated, be it mindfulness, self-compassion, or a supportive network. Acknowledging that we must sometimes navigate through darkness allows us to appreciate the light even more when it returns, and it always does – just look at how the sun rises each morning, only to set again as night time. This daily cycle serves as a powerful reminder that life is about balance, both light and darkness play integral roles in our experience. Embracing this duality helps us understand that challenges often lead to growth and renewal. Everything in life signifies this balance, teaching us that even during difficult times, there is the promise of brighter moments ahead. It's through this interplay that we cultivate resilience, find strength, and learn to navigate the waves of life with grace.

The key is to keep moving through life with intention, even when progress feels slow or even stalled. Every challenge is an opportunity to reaffirm our commitment to our journey, to dig deeper into our motivations, and to rediscover our strength. Just like eating an elephant, one bite at a time, each step, no matter how small, provided it is in the right direction, it will inevitably take us closer to our goals. Every obstacle, no matter how overwhelming it may seem in the moment, is broken down into manageable parts when we approach it with patience and persistence. As we face these challenges, it's not just about returning to normality, but about recognising that every setback offers a powerful reminder of our resilience. Each challenge is part of the process, helping us grow stronger and more self-aware. By embracing these tests, we reaffirm our desire to pursue our goals and connect with our authentic selves. Through every small step, we continue forward, flowing with the rhythm of life's waves, understanding that both the highs and lows are essential to our growth and evolution. Instead of resisting, we embrace them both, knowing that each moment, whether smooth or turbulent, shapes us into who we are meant to become. In fact, I find myself even more excited during challenging times, knowing they bring lessons, growth, and new perspectives. When I welcome them with open arms instead of resistance, they don't seem to linger as long, but rather pass through like waves, leaving wisdom in their wake. I'm here for it all - the highs, the lows, the lessons, and the growth. Every experience has its place, and I embrace each one as part of the ever-unfolding journey.

I invite you to consider: What "elephant" in your life currently feels overwhelming? What challenge or goal seems too vast to tackle? Try breaking it down into the smallest possible actions - what's the first "bite" you could take today? Remember that consistent small steps, taken with intention and patience, will eventually lead you to your destination. The journey of a thousand miles begins with a single step, and overcoming life's biggest challenges starts with a single bite. As you move forward, know that each small action not only brings you closer to your goal but also builds the strength and resilience you'll need for whatever lies ahead.

8 SELF-DIALOGUE

How frequently do we find ourselves caught up in an internal dialogue without fully even realising it, allowing our thoughts to drift, to take some sort of shape and run their own course without much input? This passive approach can often result in a counter-productive journey, potentially spiralling into negativity seeing that our minds by nature, are predisposed to a negative bias, driven by their primal role of ensuring our safety. This inherent tendency can lead us down paths of self-doubt and fear if we don't actively steer our thoughts. Instead of letting our internal conversations roam aimlessly and they generally do that as our brains are just trying to process and release all the junk we've stored in there that we have not dealt with, it's crucial to take a proactive role in shaping them. By consciously directing our self-talk towards positive and purposeful goals, we can counteract the mind's default negativity and guide ourselves towards a more constructive and authentic direction. At the same time, addressing suppressed emotions or unresolved triggers, those feelings we've avoided or buried, becomes a key part of healing and growth. Releasing the emotion attached to a memory is one way to process these feelings, but what happens when the emotion is not clearly linked to a specific memory because it has been buried so deep? When emotions aren't clearly linked to specific memories, try this step-by-step process to release them::

- First, become more aware of the present emotional experience and acknowledging it's there, as well as why it's there because emotions are always valid, but often misinterpreted. Sometimes, we may feel a certain discomfort or unease, but the origins of the emotion might feel distant or unclear. Just sit with the feeling rather than trying to avoid it, suppress it and allow yourself to observe without judgment.

- Second, practice deep, mindful breathing to create a sense of calm and presence. Focus on your breath, inhaling deeply and exhaling slowly. As you breathe, imagine the emotion as energy moving through your body. Breathe into the feeling, allowing it to dissipate with each exhale. You can also use my other visualisation technique with the cloud or any other which you find works for you.

- Third, find a healthy way to express the emotion. This

could be through physical movement (like shaking it out or stretching), creative expression (such as journaling or drawing), or whatever else it is that you can relate to. Saying the emotion or writing it down can help release its grip. Once you've created the space for the emotion, set an intention to release it. You can mentally say, "I choose to release this emotion now," or "I allow myself to let go of this feeling." Intentions help you consciously decide to release what no longer serves you, even if you don't fully understand where it came from.

-    Finally, reflect on what you've just experienced and be gentle with yourself – it is absolutely normal to have emotions. Ask yourself what you've learned from the emotion or how it may have served you. Understanding the purpose of the emotion can help you integrate the release and gain insights for future emotional growth.

Going back to our thoughts, I need to distinguish between thoughts that come from the divine, universe, God or your higher self (ultimately the same place, but I think people prefer different terminology, based on their belief system) - those we want to learn to recognise and be guided by, and thoughts that arise from your mind's habitual chatter. Higher-self thoughts come with a sense of calm, clarity, and alignment with our true values and long-term purpose, they uplift us and feel natural. In contrast, mind-generated thoughts, particularly those on autopilot, often bring stress, anxiety, or discomfort, reflecting old fears and doubts. These thoughts tend to be repetitive, forced, and misleading. For example, the voice that insists "You're not qualified for this job" despite your preparation, or "They don't really like you" without evidence, typically comes from insecurity rather than intuition. The key is learning to recognise and be guided by the former while letting go of or redirecting the latter, ensuring that the path we walk is one of truth, alignment, and deeper understanding.

The mind, ever vigilant, is tasked with the noble mission of safeguarding us by instinctively choosing the path of least resistance, drawing on past experiences and risk factors to navigate life's complexities and ultimately ensure survival. This protective mechanism, can be limiting in many ways by focusing on what has been rather than what could be and completely overlooking what is. In contrast, thoughts that flow with ease and purpose often originate from a deeper, more divine source, guiding you towards your authentic self. These inspired insights, unburdened by past limitations, encourage you to transcend old patterns and embrace a path aligned with your truest self and desires. Balancing these two forces - mind's cautious tendencies and divine guidance can help you navigate life's journey with both wisdom and purpose, leading you toward the person you aspire to be, forever learning, growing and evolving.

Addressing and overcoming negative bias involves a mindful and proactive approach to reshaping your internal dialogue. You can begin to do so by cultivating awareness of your thought patterns, noting when and why negative thoughts arise and then challenge these thoughts by questioning their validity and seeking evidence that contradicts them or practice the release technique above, or perhaps adjust such to what may better work for you. Additionally, it is crucial to address any unresolved issues from your past, particularly those related to your inner child, which may have felt hurt, neglected or overlooked. By acknowledging and healing these past wounds, you can better understand and transform the negative biases that influence your current thought processes and existing belief systems, so as to enable you to challenge same and rewrite as desired.

Reframing situations involves shifting your perspective to see challenges and setbacks as opportunities for growth and learning, rather than fixating on what went wrong or what could go wrong. This process starts by consciously challenging your initial reaction to a situation, which is often coloured by fear or negativity. Instead, try to view the situation from multiple angles: consider what skills you might develop, how you could adapt, and what positive outcomes might emerge from the experience.

For instance, if you face a professional setback, instead of dwelling on the failure, ask yourself what lessons you can learn from it, how it might lead to better strategies in the future, or how it could prompt personal growth. This shift in perspective not only reduces the emotional impact of negative events but also encourages a more constructive approach to problem-solving. By focusing on the potential for growth and the positive aspects of a situation, you reframe your mindset to be more resilient and forward-thinking, fostering a more optimistic and empowered outlook on life's challenges, which are inevitable. In my mind for example, there are no problems – only a range of solutions.

Another aspect is to incorporate gratitude practices into your routine to shift your focus from negativity to positive aspects of your life, for even in the midst of chaos there is positivity or positive aspects. By regularly acknowledging and appreciating the things you are thankful for, you actively redirect your attention towards the good in your life, which can significantly enhance your overall sense of well-being. The more grateful we are, the more we will have to be grateful for. This practice involves setting aside time each day to reflect on and write down or simply go through the list in your mind of what you are grateful for, whether big or small. I personally do this every night before going to bed, as it is a nice way to end the day on a positive note, irrespective of what went on during the day. Over time, this habit helps train your mind to recognise and value positive experiences, reducing the tendency to dwell on negative aspects. At the end of the day, there are no inherently positive or negative experiences - there are simply experiences. It is we who assign meaning to them, categorising them based on how they made us feel. Similarly, our beliefs shape our reality, which is why activated beliefs, which are intentional, empowering statements reinforced by action, can be a powerful tool in transforming our mindset. Rather than mere affirmations, these are deeply felt, embodied truths designed to rewire limiting thought patterns and instill confidence. For example, instead of just saying, "I am capable of achieving my goals," you consciously embody that belief by taking aligned action, proving it to yourself. Activated beliefs transcend the words - they require awareness, repetition, and intentional follow-through. The more we integrate them into our daily lives, the more we reshape our self-perception, reinforcing a mindset that aligns with our true potential. Activated beliefs are more than just positive statements - they're commitments to embody new ways of seeing yourself that you reinforce through deliberate action. For instance, instead of merely saying "I am confident in social situations", you would consciously practice confident body language, initiate conversations, and reflect on successful interactions afterward. This combination of affirmation plus consistent action rewires your neural pathways, gradually transforming how you perceive yourself and how you show up in the world.

Together, gratitude practices and activated beliefs form a powerful foundation for shaping a balanced and constructive internal dialogue. This approach doesn't involve tricking yourself into false positivity or ignoring reality - it's about consciously directing your focus toward what is real, meaningful, and within your control. By acknowledging genuine positives in your life and reinforcing your strengths through activated beliefs, you cultivate resilience, clarity, and a mindset rooted in growth. Paired with intentional action, this practice fosters an optimistic yet grounded outlook, allowing you to engage with challenges not from a place of fear or avoidance but from a place of confidence and adaptability.

Engaging in mindfulness and meditation can help you become more aware of your thoughts and reduce their negative impact. You don't need to be an expert to start incorporating mindfulness and meditation into your daily routine. To begin, set aside a few quiet minutes each morning to center yourself and prepare for the day. Find a comfortable spot where you won't be disturbed, and sit or lie down in a relaxed position – I sometimes do this straight from bed, as I wake up – I think it's less about whether you're standing or sitting and more about how open, aligned, and engaged your body and mind are in the moment, so however way you wish to do it, ensure you follow the main principles of alignment, intention and receptiveness. You can start with simple mindfulness practices such as focusing on your breath. Pay attention to the sensation of each inhale and exhale, and gently bring your focus back whenever your mind wanders. You can also engage in brief meditation sessions. This could involve repeating a calming phrase, such as "I am calm and cantered," or simply observing your thoughts without judgment, allowing them to come and go. As you practice, aim to create a sense of calmness and direction for the day ahead. This routine helps you become more aware of your thoughts and feelings, allowing you to notice, acknowledge and release any negative patterns before they gain momentum. Over time, these practices can reduce the negative impact of your thoughts, enhance your emotional resilience, and set a positive tone for your day.

The more we release negative emotions attached to memories or our failure to accept reality as it is, the more we reduce the constant chatter in our minds. This mental chatter often arises when we resist the present moment, cling to past hurts, or worry about future outcomes. In essence, the mind is attempting to clear the slate, to make space for clarity and peace, but when we hold onto unresolved emotions, it becomes cluttered, making it harder to focus or move forward. By consciously letting go of these emotions, whether they stem from past experiences, unfulfilled expectations, or our resistance to the way things are - we create mental and emotional space. This space allows our minds to quiet down, enabling us to think more clearly, act with intention, and approach life with greater peace. The more we practice releasing negative emotions, the more we invite stillness and presence into our lives, allowing us to respond to situations rather than react from a place of unresolved tension. The brain, in trying to clear the slate, helps us shift from a state of overwhelm to one of balance, making it easier to align with our authentic selves and the flow of life.

While these internal practices are powerful, our self-dialogue is also heavily influenced by our relationships and social environment. Surround yourself with positive, like-minded individuals who support and uplift you, and set realistic goals that build your confidence and celebrate your progress. When navigating difficult family dynamics, something nearly everyone experiences to some degree, it's essential to strike a balance between maintaining meaningful connections and setting boundaries that protect your well-being. That said, don't hesitate to distance yourself from those who consistently drain your energy, undermine your growth, or diminish your quality of life. Life is too short to endure relationships that bring constant negativity or harm. If someone repeatedly disregards your boundaries despite your efforts, stronger measures may be necessary, including limiting or even severing contact if their behavior remains toxic. Prioritising your emotional health requires discernment and courage, which means knowing when to protect your peace while ensuring your life is shaped by supportive, enriching relationships. And if cutting ties is the only way forward, then do what you must, but, if possible, do so with grace.

By integrating all of the aforementioned strategies, you can actively guide your self-dialogue towards a more balanced and optimistic perspective, harmonising the mind's protective tendencies with the divine guidance that steers you toward your authentic self.

It takes discipline, consistency and willingness to distinguish between the two thought patterns and the rest is really just practice. The more you practice, the more you get it right and the more you feel like you are on the right path, even if it is only transitional. Remember to be kind and patient with yourself and others, for everyone is fighting some sort of a battle, mainly with themselves.

Make sure all self-dialogue is serving you to its highest purpose, leading you on your desired authentic path, towards achieving your personal goals by being fully in your element, experiencing joy, lightness and peace in your heart. If not, you can change it and consciously you can recalibrate and reprogram yourself as per your desires. Ensure your desires are well thought out for it is impossible for the same person to be in a different state of being-you'd have to know which parts of yourself you're willing to let go of and set part with. Get to know yourself, get in touch with your intuition and be guided by it for this is the path you need to follow. I feel so many of us are aimlessly passing through life, getting distracted along the way and then wondering why we're even here? Feeling frustrated, anxious, irritable and snappy, struggling and living from a place of scarcity – I get it, I have been there and to this day I make conscious effort to be the person I know I am. To learn, to grow and to experience life, to accept things and people as they are and to surround ourselves with the right tribe and here, I use the term tribe very loosely. The people we attract into our lives can be influenced by both where we are in life today and the potential for growth we are open to. On one hand, we tend to attract people who resonate with our current state, beliefs, and energy. This means that the people who enter our lives often reflect our present mindset, emotional state, or circumstances. If we're in a particular phase of growth, we might attract those who mirror our current experiences or challenges, as they can help us navigate and process where we are right now. On the other hand, we also attract individuals who are aligned with the potential we hold for the next level of growth. Sometimes, the people who enter our lives may push us toward transformation - offering us the lessons, perspectives, or challenges needed to transcend to a new stage of development. These relationships may feel like they are guiding us toward something greater, helping us expand beyond our current limitations. In many ways, it's a dynamic interaction: the people in our lives reflect both where we are and where we're capable of going. If we're open to growth and willing to evolve, we can attract relationships that catalyse that transformation, even if those people are initially drawn to us because of where we are today. Our openness to learning, evolving, and embracing new perspectives ultimately shapes the kinds of relationships we form. So, it's not necessarily one or the other - it's often both, working together in a way that encourages growth at each stage of life.

Take time to still the body and mind, allowing creative energy to flow freely. In these moments of quiet, the answers you seek often reveal themselves with a strong sense of knowing. Trust this knowing, trust your intuition, even if it's not necessarily what you want to hear at that moment. This is where the alignment between where we are and where we're meant to go becomes clear. Our intuition often guides us toward the people, opportunities, and experiences that help us transcend to the next level, but sometimes, in our impatience or stubbornness, we may choose to ignore it. I recall several instances where my instinct would tell me one thing, but in my desire to get to where I thought I wanted to be faster, I chose the opposite path. My mind would push me toward what I wanted in the moment, and in doing so, I realised later that my intuition was right all along. I found myself taking a step backward instead of forward. In these moments, perhaps my desires were not aligned with my deeper beliefs or the growth that was meant for me. For example, I may have wanted something immediate, like external success or validation - without considering whether it was in harmony with my true purpose or long-term fulfilment. This alignment - between where we are now and the people or circumstances that appear in our lives - often reflects both the lessons we need and the growth we are capable of. Our intuition serves as a compass, guiding us toward connections and experiences that will help us evolve. When we trust the "knowing" and embrace the journey, even if it's not the path we originally envisioned, we start to see how everything, including the people we meet along the way, aligns with where we are meant to go. It's in this trust and surrender that we begin to attract the right people who will support us in transcending to the next level, in our relationships, external markers and in our own personal growth.

Your body only takes you where your mind is. I did discuss this already, but I will do it again, purposefully. What does that even mean? A simple concept yet not so easy to understand and in turn, implement. The key really is discipline, consistency and allowing yourself to go beyond your limited beliefs and experiences. Allowing yourself to let go of the fear of the unknown, allowing yourself to go beyond the comfort zone and push a little further into the unknown, knowing that the vibration at which you operate and function is that same vibration which will attract into your life more of that. Everything we focus on grows and becomes our reality. For example, at any point in time you have a choice to focus on one of at least two options, but for purposes of driving the point home, let's call it a problem and a solution. If a problem presents itself, or rather when it does, you have a choice to focus and overemphasize the problem itself and get stuck in it and claim the victim card or you can focus on solving it, sometimes merely by observing it pass by and not react. This concept really goes hand in hand with surrendering into the unknown. This perspective shift transforms challenges from overwhelming obstacles into opportunities for creative problem-solving, allowing you to approach difficulties with confidence rather than fear.

You hold the power of your own destiny – dare to create and to be authentically you, whichever "you" you choose to be. This means recognising that you have the power to shape your life according to your values,these desires, and dreams. Dare to pursue what truly resonates with you, making choices that align with your genuine self rather than conforming to others' expectations or limitations. By tapping into your inner strength and authenticity, you pave the way for a fulfilling and self-directed journey, crafting a life that reflects your true essence and aspirations.

Here, it's important to acknowledge that there are no shortcuts to achieving your goals and the only place you can find what you truly want is by looking inwards. You need to look deeper to understand what your goals truly mean to you and how you plan to attain them. For instance, while many people chase wealth, it's crucial to define what being "wealthy" means to you personally and create a concrete plan to achieve that vision. Consider whether immense financial success is valuable if it comes at the cost of your health, or at the cost of having genuine relationships, or at the cost of your mental well-being? There is a price to pay for overindulging in anything, every single time. Reflect on how your choices align with your overall well-being and long-term goals, ensuring that your pursuits are in harmony with your core values and contribute to a balanced, fulfilling life.

9 TRIAL AND REFINEMENT

There are no true mistakes in life - only lessons, enlightenment, and opportunities for growth and refinement. Life's challenges and setbacks are not failures: they are the universe's way of guiding us toward greater understanding and self-awareness. Each so-called mistake is an event that pushes us to explore new perspectives, test our resilience, and adapt to circumstances we might not have anticipated. These moments of "error" are where the seeds of wisdom are sown. When we embrace this mindset, we free ourselves from the paralysing grip of self-punishment, discouragement, fear and stagnancy. Viewing experiences as lessons rather than failures enables us to remain open and curious, rather than closing ourselves off to the possibilities for growth. Regression only occurs when we choose to dwell in self-criticism and allow fear or shame to block us from moving forward. This is why I prefer to see life as a process of trial and refinement rather than trial and error - the word "error" implies failure, while "refinement" acknowledges that each attempt brings us closer to mastery.

Growth comes from acknowledging that life is inherently a process of trial and refinement, as opposed to trial and error. Even in the most challenging times, there are insights to be gained if we are willing to look for them. For example, what might feel like a professional setback can teach us patience, better communication, or the value of persistence. A strained relationship can help us understand boundaries, forgiveness, or the courage to stand in our truth. Mistakes are signposts, redirecting us to paths we might not have otherwise considered or embarked on. The key lies in how we interpret and respond to these experiences. Do we see them as opportunities to evolve, or do we allow them to harden us with regret?

Ultimately, every experience, no matter how it initially appears, is a part of our story, contributing to our growth and shaping the person we are becoming. The ability to embrace life as a continuous learning journey transforms not just how we see mistakes but how we see ourselves: not as flawed, limited beings striving for perfection, but as ever-evolving unlimited beings striving to continuous growth and improvement. Mistakes are valuable because they provide us with opportunities to learn, improve, and ultimately grow by fostering adaptability and flexibility in both our thinking and actions. Mistakes indicate that we are willing to step outside our comfort zones, try new things courageously, and allow ourselves to look foolish or inexperienced at first. This is often where great things happen. If you feel scared stepping into the unknown, do so anyway - embrace the courage to move forward, and watch that fear diminish as confidence grows alongside experience. The more you practice a task, the more you learn about it and the better you become at it. Each mistake carries a lesson that can enhance your skills and understanding, provided you approach it with a mindset of growth and reflection, rather than viewing it through a negative lens, such as that of victimhood. At some point, every expert was a beginner, a learner, and before that, an infant reliant on its caregivers for survival.

Embracing mistakes as learning opportunities is the foundation of growth, but the journey to mastery requires more than just trial and error. It demands refinement, perseverance, adaptability, and the willingness to push past fear and societal expectations. What does it take to become exceptional, an expert in your field, or an innovator? The answer lies in the will and perseverance to pursue growth, paired with the ability to remain flexible in your thinking, consistent in your approach, and unphased by the opinions of others, whilst taking careful note of constructive criticism. This ability becomes especially relevant as we grow older, enabling us to explore innovative concepts without fear of failure. If failure comes, it's about taking accountability, rectifying mistakes to the extent possible, and ensuring they don't happen again, or at least not in the same way. It is essential to distinguish between negligence or lack of due diligence and honest human errors.

While the journey to mastery often demands perseverance and adaptability, it also demands that we embrace the inevitable challenges and failures along the way. This process, rooted in both accountability and resilience, is not just theoretical - it is something we all experience from our earliest years. Consider the example of a child learning to walk. What begins as an unsteady process, marked by countless falls, evolves into a skill mastered through repeated effort, growing strength, and unwavering determination. This very same principle applies to children with disability too – they find ways to overcome their challenges, adjusting and persevering to excel in the areas where they can. This fundamental principle applies universally, reminding us that cultivating a resilient and adaptable mindset is key to overcoming challenges and achieving growth, no matter the stage of life, and the set of cards we have been dealt in life. Just as the child doesn't give up after the first, tenth, or even hundredth fall, we too must approach our pursuits with patience and persistence, understanding that each "failure" is merely feedback guiding us toward improvement.

It's crucial to learn from our mistakes and, if you are truly open-minded, from the mistakes of others too. We must ensure that our mistakes do not harm others to the extent it is within our control. This includes adhering to laws, safety precautions, and ethical guidelines – all principles that are fundamentally rooted in respecting others' lives and treating them as we ourselves would wish to be treated. These are simple, yet profound, principles of life, which emphasise compassion, mindfulness, and respect for all beings. Taking responsibility for our actions involves being aware of their consequences, making amends where necessary, and reflecting on our missteps to avoid repeating them. By doing so, we contribute to creating a more positive and supportive environment, fostering both personal and professional growth along the way.

For many years, society has perpetuated the notion that making mistakes is something to be penalised, especially in high school settings. During these formative years, there was a widespread belief that grades were an accurate reflection of one's intelligence. For students whose grades didn't meet expectations, whether due to personal struggles or simply not resonating with traditional testing methods, this belief could erode their confidence and foster feelings of inadequacy. Poor marks, in this context, often feel like a personal failure, deeply embarrassing and intertwined with one's sense of self-worth. The education system, for all its strengths, often operates on the premise of "my way or the highway," which creates a dichotomy of outcomes: strong academics, strong rebels, and a middle group that neither fully thrives nor completely disengages. Very few students manage to excel in both realms, and the current structure leaves little room for diverse learning styles, personal growth, and self-expression. This rigidity can inadvertently marginalise students whose talents and ways of thinking do not align with traditional educational methods. There remains a troubling societal association between high grades and intelligence, despite the fact that these two concepts are not inherently linked. Many students who perform poorly in traditional academic settings may excel in other areas, such as creative problem-solving or innovative thinking. Yet, in a system that often values standardised responses, such talents are frequently overlooked or undervalued. Moreover, for students dealing with anxiety, fear, or adjusting to new environments, the pressure to perform in exams can become overwhelming. The focus on rote memorisation and rigid application of knowledge leaves little room for cultivating the comprehension, creative thinking, and real-world problem-solving skills that are essential for navigating life's challenges. These qualities are the foundation for personal and professional success, but the current educational system, for all its merits, often fails to nurture the flexible, adaptable mindset required for growth. Simply put – it's outdated in many ways.

Not to mention, none of it truly prepares students for real life. Practical life skills, such as financial literacy, communication, emotional intelligence, and critical thinking are often overlooked. Even when students move on to tertiary education, the system fails to provide them with the practical skills they'll need in their chosen fields. After leaving school, many students find themselves unprepared for the challenges of the real world and often quit, before they even start. While they may be able to conduct research or memorise academic content, they often lack the hands-on, real-world experience and problem-solving skills that are necessary for success in life and work.

My own educational journey illustrates many of these shortcomings and demonstrates how overcoming them requires both resilience and the ability to redefine one's relationship with "mistakes". I was one of those students who struggled in high school, feeling constantly undermined by a system that didn't seem to understand or value my way of thinking. Educators, while mostly well-intentioned, often felt unrelatable, impatient and rigid - traits that do little to inspire or encourage students. This approach is not conducive to fostering true learning or personal growth. Teachers hold a tremendous responsibility, and their role requires more than just knowledge of a subject - it demands emotional intelligence, flexibility, and the ability to relate to students with authenticity and kindness. Unfortunately, many educators lack these qualities, which can result in a disconnect that undermines their true value. To truly foster diversity and inclusivity in education, teachers must remain open to different learning styles and needs. By embracing flexibility and adaptability, educators can create environments where students feel respected and empowered to explore their strengths, even if they don't align with traditional academic expectations. Emotional intelligence plays a crucial role in this process. It allows educators to recognise the individuality of each student, acknowledging their unique challenges and talents, and helping them feel seen, heard, and valued.

Further training in emotional intelligence, empathy, and flexible teaching methods is essential. Teachers need to be equipped not only with academic knowledge but also with the tools to nurture self-awareness, creativity, and resilience in their students. This goes beyond the curriculum - it's about creating a learning environment where students are encouraged to think critically, take risks, and grow in ways that extend far beyond the classroom. Teaching is not just a job: it's a vocation that requires deep understanding, sensitivity, and a commitment to the holistic development of each student. Only then can the education system evolve to support the growth of all students, equipping them with the skills and mindset needed to navigate the complexities of life and the practicalities of the real world.

The current education system, while focused on academic achievement, often overlooks the practical skills that prepare students for the real world. Creative thinking, for instance, encourages approaching problems from different angles and fosters innovative solutions, yet it's seldom nurtured in traditional schooling. Problem-solving, another essential skill, involves analysing challenges and overcoming obstacles - preparing students for complex situations they will face in life. Self-awareness, too, is key: it helps individuals understand their strengths, weaknesses, and values, ultimately guiding informed decisions about careers and personal life choices. In addition to these, education should place greater emphasis on resilience and adaptability, teaching students how to handle failure with grace and perseverance. This quality is often overlooked, yet it's fundamental for both academic growth and personal development. Communication skills and emotional intelligence are equally critical. The ability to connect with others, understand different perspectives, and manage emotions is vital in every aspect of life. Practical skills like financial literacy, time management, and critical thinking are often sidelined but are essential for success beyond the classroom. By integrating these elements into the education system, we would equip students not just to excel academically, but to thrive in real-world environments, building a strong foundation for both professional achievement and personal fulfillment.

The reason I'm sharing all of this is because, to some extent, you may relate to what I'm saying, possibly from personal experience. You might feel like the circumstances or challenges you've faced have shaped you in ways that feel hard to overcome. But it's important to remember that, as a creator of your own story and not as a victim of your past, you possess the power to change things around at any point in your life. If you ever find yourself feeling disconnected from where you are or who you are at this moment, remember that the potential for growth and transformation is always within your reach. The journey is not about judgment, but about recognising your capacity for change and embracing the opportunity to shape your path in a way that resonates with your true self.

After finishing school, I spent a few gap years unsure of what to do - an experience that mirrored my low self-esteem and lack of direction at the time. My parents also couldn't afford to send me to university and although they could have made a plan, I didn't want them to put themselves under any more pressure. During this period, I did all sorts of odd jobs, including waitressing and one day I was fortunate to be offered a job with a private investigator who saw potential in me. His belief in my abilities led me to pursue a paralegal qualification and, just a year later, a law degree. Through this journey, I rediscovered my capabilities and realised that mistakes and challenges are not roadblocks, but stepping stones to growth. I transitioned to a law firm while studying and I was entrusted with responsibilities that pushed me far beyond my comfort zone. It was in these moments that I learned I could achieve far more than I ever thought possible. Sometimes, life sends us little reminders of what we are capable of when we have forgotten. These reminders help us reconnect with our strengths and abilities, allowing us to see ourselves in a new light. So the next time an opportunity presents itself that's worth pursuing, just grab it and you can always adjust as you go along.

What I came to understand is that mistakes are often signs of progress and growth, especially when approached with accountability and reflection. To truly move forward, it's crucial to know yourself deeply, stay true to your values, and remain open to constructive feedback, all while preserving your authenticity. Life, in many ways, has no real limits beyond those we impose on ourselves. Embracing this mindset allows us to take risks, step into the unknown, and ultimately unlock our full potential. Reprogramming your mindset and revitalising dormant skills requires effort, but the rewards can be transformative and very rewarding.

In the legal profession, as in many others, mistakes can have serious consequences and there's little room for error, which highlights the importance of mastering the fundamentals and developing a strong ethical foundation early on. Without this, poor judgment can lead to severe repercussions. However, by cultivating resilience, adaptability, and a commitment to growth, we can navigate even the most demanding environments with confidence and integrity. Ultimately, embracing challenges, learning from every experience, and evolving with each step we take allows us to reach new heights, contribute positively to the world, and continually become our best selves. This journey of growth and self-discovery is ongoing, but it is a path that we have the power to shape at any point in our lives.

And the beauty of trial and refinement is this: the more we embrace the process, the less we fear mistakes, and the more we recognise them for what they truly are - not failures, but stepping stones toward mastery. This applies to anyone, in any field. When we approach what we do with a sense of pride, integrity, and unwavering commitment, we can meet any challenge head-on and emerge stronger, more capable, and more assured in our abilities.

10 MAPPING YOUR PATHWAY, WITH PURPOSE

Many of us are unaware of our true purpose, often caught in a relentless search for something that will bring us fulfillment and a sense of completeness, that lasting satisfaction that transcends the mundane. This usually takes the form of fully investing ourselves in external factors, such as what we do, to the point where we stop being and we just keep on doing, slowly transitioning into the more accurate term for our society: "human doings". Nothing we achieve ever feels good enough. We complain about almost everything, even the simplest of things, such as the weather: how it's too hot, too cold, too wet, or just too much of something. And yet, not enough time is spent simply being and just enjoying whatever comes our way, sharing a smile, doing something kind for ourselves and those around us. Let's switch things up a bit before we end up regretting how we lived our lives and how we spent our time. We've adopted a culture of complaining, using it as a way to connect with others, but in doing so, we reinforce a habit that gradually shapes our reality. What we focus on, we amplify - so the more we complain, the more we train our minds to seek out negativity, unintentionally attracting even more to be dissatisfied with. Over time, this habit becomes our default way of thinking, influencing our perspective, our experiences, and ultimately, the life we create for ourselves. I say: never complain, never explain. It doesn't help, it doesn't ease the load: rather, it reinforces it. Let's be a little more intentional, a little more present, and a little more ourselves by shifting the status quo into a more positive realm of being where we actively seek the silver lining in everything, for there is silver lining in everything. It all begins with the way we think, the way we speak, and the way we act.

This struggle arises because we haven't taken the time to genuinely get to know ourselves - what excites us, what fulfills us, what makes us come alive. Instead, we drift through life, moving from one day to the next, one holiday to the next, with fleeting highlights scattered between long stretches of "meh" - or worse, a sense of heaviness we can't quite shake. Nothing ever feels quite enough, so we chase quick and easy feel-good fixes that often pull us even further from ourselves and our true purpose. We become trapped in fear-driven thoughts, believing we must earn prestigious titles, accumulate wealth, or meet certain societal expectations to feel worthy, to gain recognition, to matter. We tell ourselves that love must be proven to be real, that success must be measured to be valid, that our value depends on something outside of us. But in reality, self-worth is not something to be earned - it's something to be remembered. Everything we need already exists within us, and when we align with that truth, the external world naturally follows. Attract, don't chase. To access this inner reservoir of strength, love, and wisdom, we must be willing to turn inward - to sit with ourselves, to explore the depths of our thoughts, beliefs, emotions, and desires. This journey of introspection may feel uncomfortable at first, but it is the key to unlocking a more authentic, deeply rooted sense of purpose and fulfillment. And like any skill, it becomes easier with practice.

Finding your purpose begins with a deeper understanding of who you are. This journey of self-discovery is essential and requires ongoing reflection, a willingness to hold yourself accountable, and the consistency to show up for yourself, day after day. Our understanding of ourselves is constantly evolving, and just as we change and grow, so too can our sense of purpose. That's okay. Embracing this fluidity can feel daunting, and changing direction may initially seem like a setback. However, it's crucial to understand that it's never too late to pivot or reinvent yourself in a way that feels authentic and true to you. Who decided that purpose has to be tied to just one thing - one grand mission or singular quest? Purpose isn't just about the big milestones: it's woven into the smallest moments of our day. From the moment you wake up, approach even the simplest tasks with intention, such as brushing your teeth, making your bed, pausing to take a deep breath and having a cup of tea. One thing I do to snap out of autopilot and bring more awareness into my daily routine is switching things up: like brushing my teeth with my left hand instead of my right. Small changes like this help rewire the brain, breaking old patterns and encouraging presence. I also make a point to say something kind to myself whenever I look in the mirror: something that has nothing to do with appearances. After all, how we see ourselves externally is often just a reflection of our inner state of being. The more we nurture that inner world, the more naturally purpose and fulfillment flow into our lives.

You don't need anyone's permission or approval to pursue what resonates with you. Yet, many of us still feel the urge to seek validation from others. This need often stems from deep-rooted insecurities or societal conditioning that suggests we aren't enough on our own. While it's true that living in a community requires some level of conformity to shared norms, this doesn't mean sacrificing our individuality. We can engage with the world on mutually respectful terms - honoring our own beliefs and visions without infringing on those of others. It's vital to recognise that we are inherently worthy and fully capable of making decisions that serve our best interests, without doing so at the expense of others. There is plenty of goodness to go around - scarcity is nothing more than a construct of the mind. The sky was never the limit, but our mind sure is.

The journey of self-discovery involves peeling back the layers of societal expectations and fear to uncover our genuine selves. When we embrace this self-knowledge, we empower ourselves to pursue paths that align with our true values and passions, rather than those dictated by others. By letting go of the need for external validation, we open ourselves to a more authentic and fulfilling life.

To uncover your purpose, you can begin by giving yourself the space and time to genuinely get to know who you are, what you like and the unique gifts you possess that can benefit others. Gifts are meant to be shared, not kept to ourselves. Reflect on what activities or pursuits bring you joy and make you feel invested, useful and fulfilled as these are often clues to your deeper passions. Pay attention to what feels effortless and natural to you, as this can indicate areas where you might have a natural talent or calling. Consider how you can add value not only to your own life but also to the lives of others. This might involve identifying ways you can contribute to your community, make a positive impact, or support others in meaningful ways. By aligning your actions with what brings you fulfilment and serves a greater good, you start to carve out a path that reflects your true purpose and resonates deeply with your sense of self. Usually, that is not just this one thing, and this gives you the flexibility to choose the direction you wish at a particular point in your life, by electing what you focus on right now professionally versus what you focus on for fun or what you shift to later in life. At some point, your "for fun" may align with what you do professionally and perhaps this is a goal in itself.

For me, I have always had a strong sense of what is right and wrong. I've been naturally inclined to offer advice and guidance in conflict situations, speaking with conviction - yet never did I anticipate becoming a lawyer. In hindsight, however, it makes perfect sense, even if my path to it was anything but direct. Is this all that I am? Absolutely not. But it is an intrinsic part of me and my very nature which embodies a very strong sense of right and wrong, and I believe I excel at it. I have always despised limitations, and perhaps that's why life has repeatedly placed me in situations, legally or otherwise, that tested boundaries, as if urging me to do something about them.

While these principles of purpose and self-discovery apply universally, my own journey illustrates how this process unfolds in real time, with all its uncertainty, challenges, and unexpected revelations. On the 6th of February 2024, a profound sense of purpose surfaced within me - a deep knowing that I had to write this book. Even before beginning this book, I'd spent months deliberating what was next for me after emigrating to Australia, overthinking every step and clinging to control. But in truth, all I needed to do was let go and allow what was meant to emerge. Emigrating for the second time came with its own set of challenges, unknowingly stirring a deep-seated anxiety from my first experience moving to South Africa as a teenager - a transition that had been traumatic. Yet, instead of submitting to fear, I chose to look inward, to discover what would bring me true joy in this very moment of my life. I wasn't afraid to reinvent myself or, rather, to awaken a part of me that had always been there. I approached the process with an open mind, understanding that I wasn't confined to a singular path or purpose. Still, one calling stood out - an undeniable conviction to write about the journey toward authentic living, aligning with one's true nature, and sharing the insights I've accumulated over the years. My sole intention is to help others on their own path to self-discovery, challenging their thought processes, awakening what has long remained dormant or simply assisting with the momentum already gained.

By giving myself the space to confront and make peace with

my past, I came to see that every experience had been an essential piece of my story. In doing so, I opened myself to a new way of being - one rooted in trust and surrender. I learned to embrace uncertainty, taking each step without knowing exactly where the path would lead. Yet, in my heart, I knew I was headed in the right direction. This process of letting go and allowing purpose to unfold naturally has been liberating and some days terrifying, but reinforcing my belief that the journey itself holds the answers we seek.

Too often, we fixate on the destination, convincing ourselves that the outcome is all that matters. In doing so, we neglect the most important part: the journey itself and the beauty of the present moment. The process of getting there is fluid and dynamic, filled with adaptations, surprises, and challenges. Yet, it is within this process that we find growth, fulfillment, and clarity. The journey offers us direction, enjoyment, and a quiet sense of comfort, reminding us that as long as we're moving with intention and authenticity, we are exactly where we need to be at any given point in time. But think about it: when we finally get that promotion, buy that car, or move into that dream house - how long does the feeling of accomplishment and excitement last before it fades and we begin fixating on the next big thing? This endless cycle keeps us chasing fulfillment instead of living it. That's why it's crucial to find a way to enjoy the process, to be present in the moment and grateful that you are even alive, getting an opportunity to experience so many different sensations, all of which come with an opportunity for growth. Here's how we can do this with some practical steps:

1. Pause and Reflect: Set aside time regularly to acknowledge where you are and how far you've come. Create a dedicated 15-minute weekly ritual for deep, uninterrupted exploration of your progress.

2. Break It Down: Transform overwhelming goals into a "progress ladder" with each rung representing a small, achievable milestone. Celebrate each step to stay motivated and build momentum.

3. Embrace Gratitude: Practice genuine appreciation daily for both small wins and lessons learned. Don't just list gratitudes - feel them by taking a moment to absorb the sensation of appreciation after acknowledging each one.

4. Plan With Flexibility: Outline your goals while leaving room for adaptation. When plans change, try to see it as redirection rather than failure, trusting that unexpected turns have their own purpose.

5.   Incorporate Joy Daily: Don't wait for the destination to reward yourself. Find small ways to bring joy into your life each day through reflection, nutrition, movement, hobbies, or time in nature.

6.   Check Your Why: Regularly revisit your reasons for pursuing your goals to stay aligned with your deeper values and ensure your path feels meaningful.

By taking these steps as an example, we can shift our mindset from chasing fleeting accomplishments to embracing the richness of the journey. The path itself becomes the reward, and the process becomes a source of fulfillment and joy.

I will never forget an encounter from my high school days in South Africa that reinforced this very idea - that the journey holds its own value, regardless of external validation. In an English class assignment, we were asked to write an essay on any topic of our choice. After submitting mine, my mother was called into school because my teacher believed the essay was too well-written for someone like me - a child who had recently emigrated from Bulgaria and wasn't yet fluent in English. The assumption was that I must have received help. I share this story because it highlights an important truth: people make assumptions, tell themselves stories far removed from reality, and take them as fact. Yes, at the time, I had recently emigrated and still spoke with an accent (I still do), but that didn't mean I couldn't articulate my thoughts effectively on paper. Writing gave me the space to gather my ideas, structure them, and express myself in ways that speaking on the spot did not allow. It's a misconception many people have that spoken fluency is the sole indicator of one's ability to think or communicate in a language. Writing taps into a different part of us, one that is more deliberate and reflective. It's where ideas can flourish even when verbal expression feels limited. My teacher's inability to recognise this distinction wasn't just a misunderstanding of language acquisition: it was also a missed opportunity to celebrate a strength. Needless to say, she did not believe my mother either and proceeded to penalise me with a low mark for what she believed to be copyright infringement of sorts. This experience taught me an early lesson: people will misjudge your abilities based on their own biases, perspectives, and self-created narratives. But that doesn't define you. Know your strengths, own your talents, and remember: your worth is not determined by someone else's inability to see it.

This lesson extends far beyond language or writing: it applies to all aspects of life, including how we nurture our children. We need to teach them what we were never explicitly taught: how to trust their intuition, how to be in tune with themselves, and how to develop an inner compass that guides them through life whilst remaining humble. To do that though, we need to teach ourselves first, which is the part applicable across the board.

As parents, our role isn't just to love our children but to show them, through action, how to live fearlessly. A fearless mindset isn't about recklessness: it's about stepping into challenges with awareness. But how can we teach this if we're still hesitant to embody it ourselves? Growth happens when we dare to step beyond what is comfortable, when we take action despite fear. Our children learn not by what we say, but by what we do. If we want them to embrace life fully, we must first do the same ourselves.

Want to get fit? Start exercising. Want a career change? Take the steps to make it happen. Want better relationships? Strengthen the one you have with yourself first. Want to feel more at peace? Stop rushing and start being present. Whatever it is that we seek, we must model the process of pursuing it. Progress isn't about perfection: it's about getting into a rhythm and being consistent with it. Establishing consistent habits and systems, rather than focusing solely on goals, helped me tremendously in my writing journey. I had no formal training as a writer, no clear roadmap to publishing a book, but I knew I had something valuable to share. So, I started. I wrote whenever I could, knowing that getting it wrong at first didn't matter. What mattered was showing up.

And here's the beautiful part: as we raise our own frequency: our mindset, our energy - we naturally attract like-minded individuals into our lives. The thoughts we nurture will be reinforced by those around us. If we're filled with doubt, we'll find people who validate that doubt. If we move with confidence and purpose, we'll connect with others who do the same.

Everything in life is meant to flow. The moment we resist that natural flow, we create unnecessary struggle. The more we understand this, the more we can move through life with ease, responding rather than reacting. There is a certain freedom in embracing life as it is: finding gratitude not just for the highs but also for the lessons hidden in the lows. My friend Aviva embodies this beautifully, not through words but through the way she lives, reminding me that presence and acceptance are some of the greatest gifts we can give ourselves. Unbeknown to her, she helped me apply this in my own life simply by being herself. Through her presence, she reinforced in me the power of acceptance, showing me that sometimes, the most profound lessons don't come from what is said, but from what is lived.

This is where the concept of balance comes into play. Purpose doesn't have to be a grand, long-term vision. Often, we don't have that clarity right away. Instead, purpose can be found in the small, intentional acts we do each day. And just like we must first learn to trust ourselves before guiding our children, we must also learn to find purpose in our own lives before we can help others do the same. Establishing daily habits, like exercising for 15 minutes, meditating, or making small, positive impacts builds a foundation of fulfillment. Prioritising these actions, especially in the mornings when our energy is fresh, allows us to set the tone for the day. Purpose isn't just something we seek: it's something we create in how we move through our daily lives.

At its core, life operates on balance. Whether we call it karma, the Golden Mean, yin and yang, or the principle of cause and effect, every tradition recognises the same truth: what we put out into the world returns to us. In Hinduism and Buddhism, the law of karma teaches that our actions shape our experiences. Aristotle's philosophy of moderation suggests that virtue exists between extremes. Taoism speaks of flowing with the natural rhythms of life. Christianity, Judaism, and Islam all emphasise balance: whether through stewardship, justice, or moderation. Regardless of belief, the message is the same: life seeks equilibrium. Even in hardship, there is something to be gained.

This idea of balance has made me reflect on something else: could we shift the way we experience difficulties by consciously engaging in discomfort? Consider this for a moment: when we voluntarily push ourselves, whether through an ice bath, an intense workout, or tackling something mentally challenging, we may be tipping the scales in our favor. By choosing struggle on our terms, we build resilience for the inevitable struggles life throws at us. Instead of being caught off guard by hardship, we train ourselves to handle it. Over time, this might even reduce the weight of future challenges, allowing us to move through life with greater ease. Who knows? It's just a theory for now, but future generations may one day confirm it as fact. Either way, it's a form of mental and physical fitness - one that strengthens us not through mental torment but through intentional, calculated action.

Embracing discomfort is not about suffering: it's about cultivating strength. It's about meeting life with a mindset that sees obstacles as stepping stones rather than roadblocks. And in doing so, we allow more joy, flow, and balance into our lives. The hardest paths often lead to the most fulfilling destinations, but only if we have the courage to walk them.

11 BUILDING LASTING HABITS

If you think about it logically, and I am a creature of logic myself, everything is interconnected and for purposes of this chapter, I'd like to go into how the physical health and mental health are deeply intertwined. We all know how physical activity triggers the release of endorphins, which are the natural mood lifters that without fail, make us feel better than the moment before embarking on a physical activity. In addition to the feel good elements, regular exercise has been found to decrease symptoms of anxiety, depression and stress by increasing serotonin levels and improving sleep. Regular physical activity also improves our cognitive function, memory, and learning abilities, as well as the blood flow to the brain, which can enhance mental clarity and focus. All pointers suggest physical activity is good for us, so if you are not already doing it, perhaps find what you can do physically at the level of fitness you are at, and get on with it. I understand that many people have physical disabilities that vary in nature, but without fail, there would be something for everybody who wants to get active (no matter how insignificant it may seem at first) – where there is a will, there is always a way. Start walking, swimming, anything really and if you are not too sure as to what you may and may not do, you could always consult a specialist in the field or a physiotherapist who can offer guidance.

Through regular physical activity we can get better sleep and adequate sleep helps us regulate mood and cognitive function and poor sleep can exacerbate symptoms of mental health conditions. This is not to say you have such and even if you do – maybe you just need some good sleep! Good sleep supports better stress management and emotional resilience and the ability to better self-regulate. Therefore, ensure you get some quality sleep as this could be a large contributing factor to a series of other things and although I am not an expert on the topic, I surely can vouch for the difference good sleep has made on my own life and what happens when I don't, internally. As a mom of two, it feels like I have been through the ringer insofar as sleep is concerned and that naturally has had an effect on everything else and has only re-emphasised the importance of having healthy habits in place – at times I have felt dysregulated emotionally, low on energy, irritable and had very little zest for life. I've also realised that when tough times present themselves that the way I talk to myself about my sleep and energy levels has a profound impact on my overall well-being, almost creating my reality. It's true that our bodies take us to where our minds are. When I focus on negative thoughts about my sleep, it feels like I'm stuck in a cycle of stress and fatigue that just keeps spiralling. There were times when I would tell myself, "I'm just not a good sleeper anymore", so just accept it and let's get on with the current reality and that would only deepen my exhaustion and irritability, but I've started to notice that when I shift my self-talk to something that I actually desire, like reminding myself, "I'm doing my best and learning to adapt. I can sleep well again." I actually feel a difference in my energy and mood. This realisation has been a turning point for me, helping me understand the incredible power of our very own mindset in navigating the challenges of life, the challenges of being a parent and everything else. By nurturing a more compassionate and constructive inner dialogue, I'm slowly but surely making strides toward a healthier, more balanced life. It's all about recognising that what I focus on grows, and I want to cultivate a mindset that supports me, rather than holds me back.

This shift has allowed me to make healthier choices, which are my natural go to by the way, especially regarding food. When I'm tired, I often crave junk food which is really unusual for me, but by planning ahead and preparing nutritious snacks and meals, I reduce the temptation to reach for the unhealthy options.

Mindful eating has become another valuable practice for me. Before grabbing a snack, I pause to consider whether I'm truly hungry or just seeking comfort, and listen, nothing wrong with doing that now and then but don't let it become a habit. You want to cultivate healthy habits, with occasional guilt-free deviations as opposed to the former. This small moment of reflection often leads me to make more intentional choices, steering me away from mindless snacking. Creating a supportive environment around the home has been essential as well. I've limited the availability of junk food in our house, opting instead for wholesome options like fruits, nuts, seeds and if craving something sweet: dark chocolate and dates are pretty satisfactory too. Involving my kids in meal planning and preparation has not only promoted healthier eating habits for everyone around the house, but has also turned cooking into a fun, bonding experience for us, although sometimes the kids get bored and ditch me in the kitchen (just in case someone is wondering how in the world did I get that right – sometimes I do, sometimes I don't, but either way is fine as it's something I love doing).

On the note of a balanced wholesome diet, it is important for so many reasons, but some of those have to do with the essential nutrients that support brain health and function, and overall wellbeing. Omega-3 fatty acids, for instance, are linked to reduced risk of depression. Stable blood sugar levels, maintained by a healthy diet, can prevent mood swings and irritability, and I think we can all vouch for the effects on that one. Additionally, gut health plays a crucial role in this equation, as it is proven to send signals to the brain that influence our mood and mental state. If you consider for just a moment the amount of processed and sugar-enriched foods available out there on the market, sometimes even disguised as a "healthy option", you'd quickly understand why we are experiencing such high levels of dysregulated people. These foods disrupt our gut-brain connection, spike blood sugar levels, and create inflammatory responses that directly impact our mood, energy, and mental clarity. And sometimes what people really need is just some good sleep, a bit of physical exertion and a healthy snack. Ha!

It all goes both ways, our mental health in turn has a notable impact on our physical health. Chronic stress, for instance, can compromise the immune system, increasing susceptibility to illness and contributing to inflammation linked with a host of physical conditions. Individuals with good mental health are more likely to engage in self-care practices, such as regular exercise and healthy eating, and are less prone to harmful behaviours such as smoking, vaping, excessive drinking and substance abuse. Mental well-being can influence the perception of pain and affect recovery outcomes from physical illnesses or surgeries by fostering a more proactive and positive outlook.

Many studies have explored this topic, all demonstrating a positive effect. However, the exact extent of that effect remains inconsistent, which makes perfect sense when you think about it logically. The results naturally vary because they are deeply influenced by the individual and their respective belief systems, habits, and personal engagement in the process. Ultimately, what you put in is what you get out. I'm a firm believer that we create our realities by positioning our minds first: our bodies merely follow, taking us to where our minds have already arrived.

Now that we understand how deeply our physical and mental health are intertwined, let's explore how to implement this knowledge in our daily lives. To achieve optimal well-being, it's essential to adopt a holistic approach that integrates both physical and mental health practices. This involves incorporating routines that support both areas, such as combining exercise with mindfulness techniques. Regularly assessing both physical and mental health and seeking professional support where needed, such as from therapists, life coaches, dietitians, or fitness experts can ensure a balanced and comprehensive approach to health. If such are not available to you, try to tune in to your body and let that be your guide, which of course is the very best option. Engaging in self-care activities that address both physical and mental aspects, like maintaining a balanced diet, regular exercise, and effective stress management strategies, can create a robust foundation for overall well-being.

I would also like to add: don't be too hard on yourself. Liberate yourself from the need to judge or compare—whether it's yourself or others. Instead, sit with yourself and figure out who you want to be and how you intend on getting there. Make a detailed list, revisit it daily, and stick to it from an action point of view. Let it evolve as needed, allowing it to represent your vision in real time. Take daily steps, no matter how small, toward that vision. Change can happen in an instant with a single decision, but that decision must be followed by consistent actions that reinforce it.

While physical and mental health habits form the foundation of wellbeing, I've found that building lasting habits also requires addressing how we interact with others and manage our expectations - both of ourselves and those around us. In the last few years, I've experienced several personal growth spurts (I love using this phrase for us adults too) where I've made firm decisions or promises to myself that this is how things will be going forward, and I have never looked back. These changes can apply to anything: the way you think, how you conduct yourself, or what you wish to achieve. For instance, I've been battling with patience with others: particularly with those around me who don't do things the way I would, which, in my mind, is supremely efficient and without unnecessary delays. As an officer of the Court, I take things seriously and perhaps too seriously at times and I have this constant urge to be on top of everything, meticulously executing tasks the moment they arise. But this mindset can be mentally exhausting, especially when I find myself not only thinking for myself but also offering well-thought-out solutions to others, sometimes when they haven't even asked for them.

And then it hit me: what others do have nothing to do with me. We are all capable of solving our own problems, directing our own paths, and deep down, we all have the answers. So why am I so affected by the choices and timelines of others? Is it truly love that makes me want to interfere? Because if I step in uninvited, I may actually be depriving them of valuable lessons. This realisation was particularly difficult to accept as a mother. Our instinct is to fix, to protect, to remove obstacles from our children's paths. But the truth is, each person, including our children, has their own lessons to learn. Sometimes, the best thing I can do is step back, trust the process, and offer guidance only when it's sought. If I choose to do something to cater for my own obsessive nature with things being a certain way, then that's just on me, isn't it?

Of course, this doesn't mean tolerating chaos in our daily

lives. When living with others, it's absolutely normal for people to get on your nerves, but communication is key. Instead of letting frustration build, create clear schedules and set expectations for who does what. Structure allows everyone to function better, and mutual respect grows when roles are defined. If something isn't working, address it directly but calmly. The goal isn't to control others but to create an environment where everyone coexists with understanding and accountability.

Patience, I'm learning, is not just about waiting - it's about managing myself while I wait. This distinction has been transformative, shifting my focus from controlling external circumstances to cultivating inner calm regardless of what's happening around me.

This realisation has been liberating. It's a reminder that my energy is better spent focusing on my own growth and well-being rather than trying to control or influence the path of others. While I may see opportunities for improvement in their lives, it's essential to recognise that change must come from within them. If someone truly desires to make a change or move in a certain direction, there should be enough motivation within them to get started. Insofar as my kids are concerned, I want to equip them with all the possible tools so they can confidently navigate through their own lives, feeling strong and capable to solve anything that crosses their path and most importantly to never allow their own minds to cripple their way forward.

By releasing the urge to manage or direct others, I find myself feeling lighter and more at ease. It allows me to invest my time and energy into my own journey while respecting the autonomy of those around me. This shift in perspective not only enhances my patience but also fosters a sense of community and support rather than tension and frustration. Ultimately, it's about understanding that we are all on our individual journeys, and sometimes the most valuable thing I can offer is simply being there, ready to listen or support when asked, rather than trying to steer the ship myself.

Just as we must be mindful about what we put into our bodies, we must also be intentional about what information we allow into our minds. Take care of the information you choose to receive - be it from the media you consume, the movies you watch, the news you read, or the people you interact with. It's crucial to remember that your ears are not dustbins, they aren't meant to collect other people's negativity or serve as outlets for gossip. I used to allow people to express their thoughts freely and sometimes you end up in situations where you hear something you really did not want to which now involves you in someone else's issues, but I've learned to be more discerning and I am not afraid to interrupt, to gently draw their awareness to what they are doing or to simply remove myself from the conversation, depending on the circumstances. Now, the moment someone veers into gossip or negativity, I immediately intervene and redirect the conversation and turn it around. If someone has something to say about another person, especially if it's negative, I believe they should address it directly with that individual and leave me out of it. My ears are not dustbins for others' grievances. This shift in my approach has been empowering. I've found that being selective about what I allow into my mind not only protects my mental space but also fosters a more positive environment around me. You may notice that as you change your own ways and refuse to entertain the negativity of others, some people will naturally begin to fall out of your circle as they are no longer receiving out of you what they were there for. This isn't necessarily a bad thing, in fact, it can be a great thing! This doesn't mean you can't hear out a loved one vent or support them through a tough time, but at the same time, you are not to be used as a buffer. It's important to set boundaries while still being compassionate. You can listen and provide support without absorbing their negativity. By doing so, you maintain your mental clarity and well-being, allowing you to be a better friend or family member without being weighed down by their burdens. This of course applies to your immediate family and children too.

As I prioritise my well-being and surround myself with uplifting influences and like-minded people, I create space for healthier relationships that align with my values. It's a natural filtering process, where those who thrive on negativity may find it challenging to connect with someone who no longer engages in that energy. This can feel isolating at times whilst you are in the transitioning phase, but it's also a powerful reminder that personal growth often requires us to let go of what no longer serves us. Don't be scared to let go of the known when it no longer serves you.

By consciously choosing the narratives I engage with, I cultivate a mindset that encourages positivity and resilience. It's about setting boundaries not just for my interactions, but also for the media I consume. I seek out uplifting content and surround myself with individuals who inspire me to grow rather than pull me down. This intentional curation of my mental landscape has made a significant difference in my overall state of joyfulness and sense of peace.

Ultimately, this journey is about self-respect and understanding that I deserve to hear thoughts that uplift and empower me, as this is of importance to me. As I embrace this new way of living, I find that I not only feel lighter but also more capable of pursuing my goals and aspirations without the weight of others' negativity holding me back. It's a reminder that in the pursuit of growth, I must be mindful of what I allow into my life, ensuring it aligns with the person I strive to be.

12 ABUNDANCE STARTS FROM WITHIN

I believe the majority of people have been brought up from the belief that there is some or other element of scarcity, which extends far beyond any material limitations. It influences our perceptions, and overall decisions every step of the way. At its core, the belief in scarcity is the conviction that resources, whether they be in relation to time, wealth, love, or opportunity, are limited. This mindset can also extend to health - both in terms of access to healthcare and the belief that vitality and well-being are finite or predetermined. While genetics play a role in predispositions to certain conditions, research in epigenetics has shown that lifestyle choices, environment, and mindset significantly influence health outcomes. Furthermore, the availability of healthcare, nutritious food, and medical advancements can shape one's health trajectory, making it clear that health is not just a fixed resource but something that can be nurtured, expanded, and optimised with the right inputs.

The belief in scarcity can cast a shadow over our mindset, steering us towards a life of constant competition, comparison, and fear or, on the opposite end of the spectrum, into indifference, neglect, and a lack of ambition. It often breeds a sense of inadequacy and urgency, prompting individuals to hoard and protect what they have rather than share and grow, which is where the key to success lies. Others, overwhelmed by the seeming futility of it all, disengage entirely, convinced that nothing is truly within their reach. Scarcity, however, is nothing more than a perception, not an absolute reality. While the world has finite resources, it is also abundant in its potential for growth, innovation, and transformation. This dichotomy is where our mindset plays a crucial role. By embracing an abundance mindset - the belief that there is enough to go around and that opportunities can be created, we shift our mindset from limitation to infinite possibility, opening ourselves to new ways of thinking, living, and thriving. This shift in perspective extends beyond wealth and opportunities, and directly impacts our physical health as well. When we cultivate the right mindset, we set the foundation for better habits, self-discipline, appreciation of the present moment and a deeper awareness of how we treat our bodies. Our physical well-being is a reflection of our inner state: when we position our minds for growth, balance, and resilience, our bodies follow suit. True balance is found not in the extremes of scarcity or indifference, but in recognising that fulfillment, both mental and physical, is cultivated through intentional action, perspective, and alignment.

The abundance mindset aligns with many philosophical and ethical teachings that emphasise interconnectedness and the inherent value of every individual. It suggests that by giving freely and contributing positively to the world, we not only enrich others, but also ourselves. This perspective can infuse one's life with a sense of purpose and fulfilment that transcends mere material success.

On a personal level, embracing an abundant mindset can alleviate the stress and anxiety associated with a scarcity-driven existence. It encourages us to focus on what we have rather than what we lack, to appreciate the present moment, and to trust in the process of growth and change. This shift can lead to a more balanced and fulfilling life.

Sometimes, deeply troublesome backgrounds or the absence of say a parental figure can create an imbalance, leaving behind a lingering sense of rejection. But the truth is, you don't need any of that to define you. In fact, it may even be a blessing that certain people are not part of your life. Perhaps their absence shaped your resilience, your drive, and your ability to carve your own path. It's time to make peace with it all and to release what was and embrace what is, knowing that your strength was forged in the very spaces where others were absent, unavailable or didn't otherwise show up as needed. We all have the ability to create or manifest anything that we can realistically envision and truly believe we deserve for ourselves. I emphasize "realistically" here - I'm talking about things that actually exist within the realm of human possibility, not fantasy elements like growing fairy wings. This manifestation ability is rooted in our belief systems around self-worth, which may need conscious adjustment. This, in a way, ties into our existing belief systems around self-worth, which may need some adjustment. When we are in alignment with ourselves and our inner knowing is activated, it guides us in the ways needed to realise our respective visions. And when we practice genuine gratitude, we naturally attract more of what we are grateful for and more to be grateful for. Anything we focus our attention on grows and multiplies, and I firmly believe that the only real limitations in life are the ones we place upon ourselves.

Wishing for a different life and constantly fantasising about an ideal future isn't enough to create meaningful change. In fact, it often does the opposite - keeping you stuck in a cycle of dissatisfaction, unintentionally reinforcing a belief that you are incapable of achieving those visions. The lack of appreciation for the present only magnifies the gap between where you are and where you want to be. Instead of just wishing, it's crucial to take intentional, proactive steps. This means setting clear, actionable objectives and following through with a structured plan. Relying on luck alone, whether it's playing the lottery, hoping for a windfall, or expecting external circumstances to change, is not only unrealistic but also disempowering. Wishing for change is passive: taking action is transformative. True change happens when your mindset aligns with the life you envision, and your actions reflect that belief as if it has already become your reality. This is an additional layer to a positive mindset: one that goes beyond mere optimism and penetrates deeper into our belief system. Not to encourage delusional thinking, but rather to acknowledge the possibility of attaining what once seemed unreachable. There are no proven studies on the topic yet that I am aware of, but emphasis is on yet. And, realistically, some things may not be so easy to prove. But history has shown time and again that the impossible becomes possible when the mind is unwaveringly committed. Whether it's overcoming obstacles, defying expectations, or shifting what we thought was inevitable, we are often far more capable than we realise. This applies to every area of life: our physical health, our emotional well-being, and even the lessons we take from the most challenging experiences. When we fight against life, we create resistance. But when we acknowledge the lessons hidden within our struggles, surrender to the greater flow, and consciously choose how we want to move forward, we step into a different kind of power. This isn't about blind faith: it's about choosing to act with intention and refusing to be confined by limitations, whether imposed by society, circumstance, or even ourselves. We don't have to be another statistic. We can break the mold. And if nothing else, we can take what we have learned and implement it in a way that transforms the time we do have into something meaningful.

For example, when someone dreams of owning a house in a serene forest in France, what are they really longing for? Is it the house itself, or is it the sense of peace, simplicity, and fulfillment they imagine it would bring into their lives? Material wealth, while not inherently bad, is rarely the answer to deeper existential questions. The truth is, you won't find peace in the forest unless you take it there with you. This is why introspection matters. If you don't cultivate that sense of inner peace and contentment now, its absence will show up in every area of your life, no matter how much you achieve externally. The pursuit of success without balance, self-awareness, and respect for your physical and emotional well-being often leads to an inevitable crash. So, think deeply about what it is you truly want. Strip away the illusions, the distractions, the external markers of success, and ask yourself: What am I really seeking? When you find that answer, let your actions reflect it.

Lack of balance manifests in many ways: chronic stress, poor sleep, irritability, and even a sense of detachment from oneself and others - these are the body's way of signaling an internal misalignment. Over time, this compounds into more serious issues, such as burnout, anxiety, depression, and a host of physical and/or mental ailments. Poor diet, lack of movement, and a relentless work ethic with no room for restoration weaken the body, making us vulnerable to illness. And here's the sobering truth: you can have hundreds of problems in life, but the moment you have a serious health problem, you suddenly have only one. Nothing else matters when your body is failing you.

Ignoring the body's needs for rest, proper nourishment, and care turns the very vessel that carries us through life into a source of suffering. And yet, so many realise this when the damage has already been done. The irony is that the energy, wealth, and time we sacrificed for external pursuits eventually have to be redirected toward trying to regain our health. But by then, it's often an uphill battle. But the good news is, it's never too late to turn things around. By shifting our mindset toward abundance and recognising that we have the ability to create, to improve, and to align ourselves with what truly matters, we regain control. This starts from within, by focusing on presence, gratitude, and respecting both our mental and physical well-being. Someone very special to me is walking this path right now, and I believe in her unwavering willpower to reclaim her life: not just to heal, but to thrive, to defy the odds, and to prove that no story is finished until we decide it is. You are not a statistic!

This is why true success isn't just about what we accumulate or achieve, but rather it's about how well we sustain ourselves along the way. Prioritising balance, listening to our bodies, and making space for introspection shouldn't be treated as a luxury, but as a necessity. Because a thriving mind can only exist in a body that is taken care of, and a meaningful life can only be built on a foundation of well-being. In order to foster inner peace, it's essential to shift our focus from external achievements to internal growth. I am not suggesting it's one or the other - inner peace and material pursuits can of course coexist, and understanding how they interact is crucial. Material gains often bring immediate gratification and can enhance our lives in practical ways, such as providing comfort, experiences, security, and opportunities. However, if we become overly fixated on these external achievements, they can easily lead to stress, anxiety, and a sense of emptiness. For instance, the pursuit of wealth or status may encourage us to chase after goals that are not aligned with our core values and perhaps even go completely against them. This misalignment can create internal conflict, as we may achieve material success but still feel unfulfilled, possibly ashamed or guilty too. Then your attachment to that external feeling comes with the pressure to maintain or surpass that success, which can generate constant stress, leading to a cycle where we're never satisfied, no matter how much we acquire. How much is enough? On the other hand, cultivating inner peace allows us to approach material and other pursuits with a clearer perspective. When we're grounded in a sense of tranquility, we can evaluate what we truly want versus what we feel we "should" want. This reflection helps us make choices that resonate more authentically with our values and long-term satisfaction, rather than simply responding to societal pressures. A strong sense of inner peace can help mitigate the stress that often accompanies the pursuit of material success. When challenges arise, and they certainly will, such as setbacks in our career, financial difficulties, ill health or loss, your inner peace will be there to maintain your composure in the form of a resilient foundation, allowing you to respond thoughtfully rather than react impulsively, panic, spiralling into negativity which has the effect of attracting more to be ungrateful for. This resilience can lead to better decision-making and ultimately a more balanced approach to both personal and professional aspirations.

As we find more inner peace through alignment with our authentic, higher selves, our pursuits may become more aligned with our authentic selves, and as we make more mindful choices in our life, we create an environment that supports our inner tranquility. This interplay can create a very fulfilling life where both aspects complement each other rather than compete for our attention.

These philosophical perspectives on abundance mindset gain practical power when applied to our everyday interactions and choices. One of the most important applications is in how we establish and maintain our personal boundaries. What if you, too, could be your authentic self? What if… you knew who you truly are and recognised your worth to the point where nothing and no one could shake you: only inspire your growth and evolution? That includes setting healthy boundaries in your interactions and distancing yourself from those who consistently fail to honor them. A boundary is a personal limit we set to protect our well-being, values, and energy. It defines what is acceptable and what is not in our interactions with others. The biggest misconception people have about boundaries is that they are a way to control or change someone else's behavior. In reality, a boundary isn't about demanding that someone act differently: it's about deciding what you will do in response to certain behaviors. For example, saying, "You need to stop speaking to me like that!" is not a boundary, but a request that is aimed to control someone else's actions. A boundary, instead, would sound something more like this: "If you continue to speak to me disrespectfully, I will remove myself from the conversation." Notice the difference? The first statement expects the other person to change, while the second empowers you to take action based on your own limits. Boundaries are not about controlling others: they are about honoring and protecting yourself.

As we cultivate this balanced relationship between inner peace and our external pursuits, an important question emerges: what might life look like if we fully embraced our authentic selves and released the limitations we've placed on our own potential?

What if… you spoke to yourself with love and kindness, always, and actually meant it? Don't be so hard on yourself and give yourself the kindness, patience and love that maybe you didn't receive. Give yourself the same compassion and understanding you so freely offer to those you care about. Kindness truly begins within and radiates outward, shaping not only our relationship with ourselves but also with others. When we cultivate kindness at home, through self-care, patience, and understanding, we build a strong foundation for how we interact with the world. Everyone is facing their own struggles, often hidden from view, and a simple act of kindness can have a profound impact. By nurturing our own well-being and filling our own "cup," we become better equipped to offer support and compassion to those around us: loved ones and strangers alike.

This not only enriches our personal relationships but also contributes to a more connected, empathetic, and resilient society. In a world where challenges abound, the ripple effect of kindness can create a more compassionate environment for all.

What if… you embraced everything that came your way, including challenges, pain, and suffering: not as burdens to resist but as opportunities to grow, learn, and understand yourself more deeply? There is a lesson in every experience.

What if… you saw things exactly as they are, without attaching yourself to them and without layering them with unnecessary positive or negative bias? No need to overthink, to cloud your mind with imagined scenarios, or to let the past or future rob you of the moment in front of you. Only by being fully present can we truly savor life and its infinite gifts, no matter their form.

What if… we did the inner work necessary to make life with ourselves what it was always meant to be: free of bias, free of judgment, free of fear? Just free. Abundant. Limitless.

What if, indeed? Your vision paints a picture of profound self-awareness and acceptance. It's a life where the focus shifts from inner conflict, external validation, and control to inner harmony, growth, and true fulfillment. Living this way isn't necessarily easy at first: it requires ongoing effort and refinement, self-reflection, and a willingness to break free from old patterns. But the journey toward this level of self-awareness and acceptance is one worth taking, as it leads to a life rich with understanding, purpose, and genuine connections. Conscious habit creation is of paramount importance. The good news? You don't have to be flawless. Growth isn't about perfection: it's about consistency. You will make mistakes, and that's okay. Every small effort, every moment of self-awareness, every act of self-compassion adds up, shaping the foundation of a life that is deeply aligned with who you truly are. The habits that last are not the ones forced upon you, but those that become second nature, ingrained in the essence of your being. And when that happens, the need for external validation dissolves, replaced by an unwavering sense of inner peace: because you are finally, unapologetically, yourself.

Writing your reflections, learnings, and visions helps crystallise your thoughts and clarify your goals, turning abstract desires into tangible realities. By documenting your ideas, you transform aspirations into structured, actionable steps, making the path forward more intentional and achievable. But this process isn't just about the destination: it's about embracing the journey itself, finding joy in each step, learning from challenges, and appreciating the growth along the way. Creative expression, whether through writing, art, music, or any other form, enhances this process by giving shape to your inner world. It allows you to externalise emotions, process experiences, and gain deeper insight into yourself. These outlets not only foster self-awareness and accountability but also make personal growth a more engaging and fulfilling experience. By integrating both structured reflection and creative exploration, you cultivate a richer connection with yourself and a greater appreciation for the unfolding journey of becoming.

Most importantly, I'll teach my body, emotionally, mentally, and physically, to embody the feelings of fulfillment, peace, and abundance now, rather than waiting for external circumstances to dictate them. This begins with appreciating what I have today. It's not about resisting the present but fully embracing it with gratitude while aligning myself with the future I believe is within reach. That's what works for me, and it may work for you too. The shift is immediate, transforming not just what you have, but how you feel and move through life.

The journey toward abundance begins within, with a fundamental shift in how we perceive ourselves and the world around us. By releasing scarcity-based thinking, aligning our actions with our authentic values, setting healthy boundaries, and embracing both challenges and joys as part of our growth, we open ourselves to the natural flow of abundance in all its forms.

Remember that abundance isn't just about material wealth - it encompasses richness of experience, depth of relationships, clarity of purpose, and wholeness of being. As you integrate these principles into your daily life, you'll find that abundance isn't something you chase but something you cultivate and eventually embody. The seeds of abundance are already within you, waiting only for your conscious attention and care to flourish.

13 DON'T CARRY WHAT ISN'T YOURS TO CARRY

Safe to say that each individual is often engaged in their own internal battles, and we frequently find ourselves grappling with the challenge of setting and enforcing boundaries. I did discuss what a healthy boundary looks like in the previous chapter, for reference purposes. This intricate dance requires us to remain compassionate while also avoiding the pitfalls of absorbing others' problems as our own. In this context, the ability to empathise can be both a profound gift and a daunting curse, when we do not know how to protect our inner solitude. It allows us to connect deeply with others, offering support and understanding, yet it can also lead to emotional overwhelm if we're not careful and mindful. Balancing this empathy with self-awareness and boundaries is essential as it enables us to nurture our relationships without losing sight of our own emotional well-being, which is of paramount importance. Ultimately, navigating this landscape requires not only sensitivity to the experiences of others but also and foremost, a commitment to safeguarding our own mental and emotional health. For those of us who identify as empaths, feeling the pain and joy of others can be overwhelming at times as we feel it so acutely, as if it's our own. We often find ourselves deeply affected by the struggles of friends, family, and sometimes even strangers. The desire to help, to fix, and to support can be so strong that we risk losing ourselves in the process. Here, I'd like to take a deep dive into the topic of how to maintain our emotional well-being through healthy boundaries while still offering compassion and support to those around us. Speaking from experience.

It's crucial to recognise that while our intention to help are noble, it doesn't always serve the best interests of those we aim to support. The first step in managing this balance is awareness. Becoming aware of our own emotional responses to others' distress helps us differentiate between our feelings and those of the people around us. This awareness allows us to identify when we are stepping into emotional absorption rather than healthy empathy and very importantly differentiating between what is within our control and what isn't.

One of the most powerful tools an empath can employ is the establishment of boundaries. Boundaries are essential for maintaining our emotional health and ensuring that we do not become entangled in others' problems. Setting boundaries doesn't mean shutting ourselves off from those in need, but rather, it's about creating a safe space where we can offer support without compromising our own well-being along the way. Consider what healthy boundaries look like in practice for you. It may involve limiting the time you spend discussing someone's problems or choosing to engage in conversations that uplift rather than drag you down. You can still be present and supportive without delving deep into their emotional turmoil to the point of absorption.

As we navigate our empathic nature, self-care becomes a non-negotiable aspect of our lives. Caring for others is a beautiful thing, but it must be balanced with nurturing our own emotional needs at the forefront. Engaging in self-care routines, whether through meditation, exercise, quality sleep, hobbies, or quiet reflection helps us recharge our spirits and maintain our emotional resilience. Additionally, self-care allows us to process our feelings and develop coping mechanisms for when we encounter distressing situations ourselves. Journaling can be a helpful practice too, offering a safe outlet for our emotions and thoughts, and offering perspective through reflection. When I'm grappling with something really difficult, I write down my feelings, and sometimes I even burn the paper. These words aren't meant for anyone else - they exist solely to help me let go, symbolising a release and an end to those emotions. This practice has been particularly meaningful to me, as I used it to teach my oldest daughter about the importance of letting go. She has a tendency to hold onto emotions, and I wanted to show her, in a hands-on way, what it means to release them. This method is one of many that can work just as well. Find one that resonates with you and use it. With time and practice, you may find yourself able to release emotions without the use of symbolic tools, but just with your mind alone. If you're already doing that, fantastic, keep going. I've shared this practice with my older daughter in moments when she feels overwhelmed by her emotions. I hand her a piece of paper and encourage her to scribble down her grumpy or angry thoughts, or even just to scrunch the paper tightly in her hands, pouring all her emotions into it. When she says she's finished, I gently suggest she keep going a bit longer, as there's often a little more emotion left to release.

The act of transferring her feelings onto paper helps her understand the value of not holding onto emotions. It allows her to experience them fully without letting them take control. Once she's done, we take a moment to pause and reflect on what she's written or scrunched. Then, we might burn the paper together, watching the smoke rise and visualising those emotions drifting away. The ritual brings a sense of calm and closure, a tangible reminder that emotions, no matter how intense, are temporary. They are not meant to be held onto but rather experienced and released, even the joyful ones that make our hearts feel full.

By engaging in this practice, we reinforce the idea that it's okay to feel deeply and then let go. Through these rituals, we articulate our emotions, gain clarity about our emotional responsibilities, and cultivate resilience. This process teaches us that while emotions are natural and valid, releasing them creates space for new experiences and feelings to emerge. It's a simple yet profound reminder of our ability to support ourselves and others with understanding and grace.

My past tendencies to hold onto certain emotions or beliefs are closely tied to past experiences that resurface from time to time. While teaching my daughters these techniques has been rewarding, I recognize that my own journey with emotional management continues to evolve as I confront deeper patterns within myself. As I work to unravel my reactions, feelings and past beliefs in response to current situations, I often find them at odds with the person I aspire to be and believe that I am. These reactions emerge without a clear reason, yet they feel deeply rooted, stemming from wounds that may appear petty on the surface. However, it's essential to pay attention to these feelings and be aware of yourself, free of judgement. By looking for answers within, I can explore why I feel or react in certain ways and where do these beliefs stem from and are they even mine. Only by digging to the root of these emotions can I begin to release what has been holding me back, keeping me on high alert, or otherwise misaligned with my true self. As you start this process, you may discover that many of the burdens you carry have never truly been yours to bear. Often, we absorb the emotions and expectations of others, mistakenly believing they are our own. Many of us carry the misconception that we must cling to our emotions, whether out of fear, attachment, or the belief that they define us. Recognising that we are not meant to hold onto these feelings is crucial - emotions are meant to be experienced and released, not stored indefinitely. If you find yourself feeling a particular way just thinking about certain experiences, it might be a sign that you too need to release such. Learning to navigate this process involves acknowledging our emotions without judgment, allowing ourselves to feel them fully before releasing them. By embracing this perspective, we can free ourselves from the weight of unprocessed feelings, making room for healing and personal growth. Ultimately, understanding that it's okay to release emotions can empower us to move forward with a lighter heart, breaking free from the cycle of conflict and moving toward the most authentic version of ourselves, without the constant need to be on high alert at all times. This heightened state of alertness is something I'm intimately familiar with.

Coming from South Africa, where I've faced life-threatening situations, been held at gunpoint more than once, and witnessed lawlessness and corruption at every level, I developed a necessary hypervigilance. I learned to pay close attention to my surroundings and rely on subtle cues people give - the ones that often contradict their words. This survival mechanism served me well in dangerous environments, but I've had to consciously recalibrate it in safer settings, learning to trust my intuition without remaining in constant fight-or-flight mode.

When someone we care about is in distress, our instinct is often to dive in, take on their problems, and try to fix everything for them. However, true support comes not from carrying their burdens but from offering compassion: being present, listening, validating their feelings, and encouraging them without assuming responsibility for their challenges.

Everyone has the capacity to navigate their own difficulties, even if it may not seem so in the moment. Yet, people often make choices, overlook cues, and disregard personal patterns, sometimes knowingly placing themselves in difficult situations, whether in relationships or other aspects of life.

Instead of relying on external solutions or avoiding discomfort, they can learn to tap into their own inner wisdom and problem-solving abilities, which are always there, waiting to be activated. By stepping back, we allow them the space to process, explore their emotions, and take ownership of their path forward.

More often than not, people get stuck not in knowing what to do, but in taking the necessary action to do it. Taking action, no matter how insignificant it may seem, even when you don't feel ready, is the key to progress. Growth happens through doing, not waiting for the perfect moment. Support others with compassion, not by solving their problems - everyone has the capacity to navigate their own challenges. Clarity and momentum come from movement, and personal transformation begins with small, consistent steps. Trust yourself, take action, and align with the life you believe is possible.

One of the hardest lessons for empaths I suppose is probably to learn to recognise when to step back. It's easy to become overly involved, especially when emotions run high and when it concerns someone you deeply care for. However, sometimes the most compassionate action is to distance ourselves, allowing others the opportunity to navigate their own difficulties. It's essential to assess whether our involvement is genuinely helpful or if it perpetuates a cycle of dependency. Ask yourself: Is this person seeking support or simply using me as an emotional sounding board? If the latter, it may be time to gently reinforce your boundaries and encourage them to seek their own solutions.

Negative emotions are highly contagious, especially with loved ones, because our brains are wired to mirror emotions, respond to stress signals, and sync with those we care about. I've experienced this phenomenon firsthand in my closest relationships. When someone I love is anxious or upset, I often find myself absorbing that energy almost instantly, sometimes before they've even verbalised their feelings.

The fight-or-flight response, emotional investment, and personal triggers amplify this effect, making us react instinctively rather than intentionally. I've also noticed that the more in tune I am with myself, the more susceptible I am to picking up even the subtlest cues of these emotions, which means I have to maintain a constant state of awareness to stay in check with myself.

To break this cycle, I've developed practical strategies that help me maintain my emotional boundaries. When I notice myself starting to mirror someone else's distress, I pause before reacting, take a few deep breaths to ground myself, and mentally create some space between their emotions and mine. I remind myself that I can empathise without absorbing, and consciously shift the emotional energy through calm communication and awareness. It's challenging work, requiring constant vigilance and practice, but the ability to remain present for others without taking on their emotional burden is worth the effort.

Learning to let go of the emotional weight of others' struggles is perhaps the most liberating aspect of being an empath. Just because someone is suffering doesn't mean we have to carry their burden and suffer too. It's vital to understand that everyone is capable of facing their challenges, even if the process is difficult, and it usually is. Letting go doesn't mean we stop caring or that we stop loving, but rather, it's an acknowledgment that we cannot fix everything and we are not meant to either. By releasing the need to absorb others' pain, we can cultivate a more profound sense of compassion that allows us to support without losing ourselves.

As empaths, we have a responsibility to pass on these lessons to the next generation. My oldest daughter embodies the traits of a sensitive soul, often feeling the weight of fairness and injustice acutely. It's essential to guide her in developing her emotional resilience while still nurturing her empathic nature. I teach her to recognise her feelings, understand the importance of setting boundaries, and to embrace self-care. By doing so, she can learn to be there for others without compromising her own emotional well-being, her values or make poor choices. This balance will empower her to navigate her world with confidence, allowing her to offer genuine support while maintaining her inner peace. My youngest daughter is already a master of this and we can all learn from her.

The journey of being an empath is one of deep emotional understanding, yet it requires the discipline and strength to protect our own well-being. By cultivating awareness, establishing boundaries, and practicing self-care, we can engage with the world compassionately without becoming overwhelmed by it. As we learn to navigate our empathic nature, we not only enhance our lives but also create space for others to grow and thrive independently. Remember the central message: don't carry what isn't yours to carry. This wisdom allows us to become beacons of light, illuminating the path for those in need without losing sight of our own journey. The art of detachment, when practiced with love and intention, allows us to connect deeply while remaining grounded in our own truth - free from the weight of burdens that were never ours to bear in the first place.

14 CONCLUSIONS

If I've managed to share even one insight that resonates with you or inspires you to take action, then I feel my purpose has been fulfilled. My aim was to help remind you of the strength, power, and wisdom already accessible within you - not to present something entirely new, but perhaps to reawaken what has been forgotten or neglected.

Transformation can happen in an instant with awareness and intent. I believe in you because believing in you means I believe in myself, and I certainly do. We are all interconnected souls with unlimited potential and access to abundance in every aspect of our lives. We need only to activate these possibilities by first knowing ourselves deeply.

Here's to your journey ahead - may it be joyful, insightful, and invigorating! You are stronger and more capable than you realise.

Trust your resilience, take decisive action, and step boldly into the life that awaits you.

I. KEY PRINCIPLES

Core Principle	Description	Practical Applications
Discover Your True Self	The journey begins with finding who you truly are beneath conditioning and expectations.	• Regularly ask yourself "Who am I?" beyond roles and achievements and ensure your actions align • Make time for quiet reflection to receive your inner wisdom • Identify your core values and use them as your decision-making compass • Challenge limiting beliefs that restrict your growth • Remember: Your past experiences shape but don't define you
Create Your Own Reality	You are the architect of your experience through your thoughts, beliefs, and perceptions.	• Monitor your thoughts through constant check-ins: they become your feelings, actions, and reality • Direct your attention wisely, because where focus goes, energy flows • Align your thoughts, beliefs, words, and actions in the same direction • Transform your "I have to" into "I get to" to shift from victim to creator • Recognize that your

Core Principle	Description	Practical Applications
		beliefs are reaffirmed by what you attract into your life
Honor Your Physical Wellbeing	Your body is the vessel for your journey: treat it with care and respect.	• Prioritize physical movement that brings you joy and longevity • Recognize how mental health and physical health are deeply intertwined • Nourish your body with wholesome foods that support your energy • Ensure adequate sleep as a foundation for emotional regulation • Remember: When health is compromised, everything else becomes secondary
Use Emotions as Guidance & Master Self-Regulation	Your emotions serve as internal compasses:learn to navigate them skillfully.	• Recognize emotions as valuable messengers, not problems to suppress • Understand that emotions last approximately 90 seconds unless prolonged by your thoughts • Pause and breathe when triggered, asking "Why am I responding this way?" • Distinguish between your emotions and those you may be absorbing from others • Practice visualization

Core Principle	Description	Practical Applications
		techniques, seeing emotions as clouds passing in the sky • Establish personal rituals to return to center when emotionally dysregulated • Remember: All emotions are positive when appropriate and allowed to complete their cycle
Embrace Present Moment Awareness	True freedom comes from living in the now, not in hopes or fears about the future.	• Recognize that hope and fear are interconnected: both pull you from the present • Notice when you're attaching to specific outcomes, creating rigidity in your thinking • Practice flexibility by letting go of how things "should" unfold • Remember that present moment awareness allows for adaptability and flow • Understand that being present isn't passive: it's the most powerful position from which to create
Peel Back the Layers	Uncover your authentic self by addressing past conditioning.	• Keep a journal to identify emotional patterns and triggers • Speak to your inner child with compassion

Core Principle	Description	Practical Applications
		when triggered • Practice clearing your "emotional wastebasket" of suppressed feelings • Acknowledge all parts of yourself, including those shaped by difficult experiences • Recognize when you're operating from old programming versus present awareness
Embrace Transformation	Change is inevitable: resistance creates suffering, acceptance fosters growth.	• Step outside your comfort zone regularly in small ways • Reframe setbacks as "school fees" paid for valuable lessons • Practice stillness to loosen your mental grip on outcomes • Ask yourself: "What would I do if fear didn't exist here?" • View life changes as a metamorphosis: like a caterpillar becoming a butterfly • Approach the unknown with excitement: what you want lies on the other side of fear
Establish Healthy Boundaries	Define what's acceptable in your life while maintaining	• Structure boundaries as "If this happens, I will do this" rather than controlling others

Core Principle	Description	Practical Applications
	compassion.	• Remember that boundaries protect your energy, not manipulate others • Check in with yourself: "Does this act of kindness align with me?" • Know who you can open up to and who you shouldn't: not everyone deserves your vulnerability • Understand that your time, energy and vulnerability are valuable: not everyone is deserving of them
Surrender to Life's Flow	Trust the process without needing to control every detail.	• Notice when you're forcing situations and consciously relax • Distinguish between divine guidance (calm) and anxious overthinking (stress) • Know when to step back and when to push harder when facing resistance • Accept what is while working toward what could be • Understand that surrender isn't giving up - it's being open to possibilities beyond your limited vision

Core Principle	Description	Practical Applications
Release Emotional Attachments	Emotions are meant to flow through you, not be held onto indefinitely.	• Allow yourself to fully feel emotions without judgment • Recognize when you're clinging to past hurts or resentments • Practice letting go through physical movement, writing, or visualization • Set intentions to release emotions that no longer serve you • Remember: Clinging to both negative and positive emotions restricts your natural flow
Take One Bite at a Time	Break down challenges into manageable steps and focus on the process.	• Divide overwhelming goals into small, achievable tasks • Track your progress visually to stay motivated • Celebrate small victories along the way • Choose the kind of "tough" you're willing to endure for meaningful outcomes • Focus on the process rather than fixating on outcomes
Master Your Inner Dialogue	Speak to yourself with the kindness you'd offer a dear friend.	• Practice mindfulness to observe thoughts without judgment • Replace negative self-talk with compassionate

Core Principle	Description	Practical Applications
		affirmations • Surround yourself with positive influences • Be selective about the information you allow in: your ears are not rubbish bins • End each day by noting a few specific things you're grateful for • Distinguish between higher-self thoughts (calm, clear) and mind-generated chatter (anxious, repetitive)
Nurture Your Inner Child	Heal past wounds by connecting with the child within.	• Acknowledge what your inner child needed but didn't receive • Offer yourself the understanding and validation you longed for • Recognize when current reactions stem from childhood experiences, acknowledge, accept and release • Create safe spaces to express emotions your younger self couldn't • Understand that your inner child did its best with the resources available • Be the parent to yourself that you always needed

Core Principle	Description	Practical Applications
Learn from Every Challenge	There are no mistakes, only opportunities for growth and refinement.	• After setbacks, identify specific lessons learned • Practice accountability without self-punishment • Test limiting beliefs with small "behavioral experiments" • Remember that mastery comes through consistent practice • Approach life as trial and refinement rather than trial and error
Live with Purpose	Align your actions with your values and celebrate the journey.	• Regularly reflect on what brings you genuine joy • Identify your unique gifts and how they can be of service to others • Make purpose about daily intentional acts, not just grand visions • Stay flexible in approach while remaining firm in direction • See everyone and everything as a potential teacher
Cultivate Abundance Within	Shift from scarcity to abundance by discovering inner peace.	• Challenge scarcity beliefs with awareness of the present moment • Practice gratitude for what you have while working toward what you desire • Take proactive steps

Core Principle	Description	Practical Applications
		rather than passively wishing • Identify what you truly want beyond material possessions • Remember: true peace can't be found externally - you can't find peace in the forest unless you take it there with you
Reshape Your Belief Systems	You can transform your experience by changing how you define concepts in your mind.	• Examine the words you use and the meanings you've assigned to them • Redefine words like "change," "growth," and "uncertainty" to transform your relationship with them • Choose words that empower rather than diminish your experience • Notice how your language shapes your perception and actions • Remember: Changing your definitions changes your reality
Find Inner Calm & Joy Without External Reason	True peace and happiness exist within, independent of circumstances.	• Recognize that inner peace and joy don't require external circumstances • Understand that this state of being is your natural birthright • Practice experiencing joy and calm for no

Core Principle	Description	Practical Applications
		particular reason • Notice when you're waiting for conditions to be "right" before allowing happiness • Remember: You'll know you're on the right path when you feel inner calm arising spontaneously
Embrace Vulnerability as Strength	Your deepest sensitivities are also your greatest powers.	• Recognize that your vulnerabilities are actually your greatest strengths • Understand that feeling deeply is both a vulnerability and a gateway to connection • Practice selective vulnerability - sharing your authentic self with those who have earned it • See emotional openness as courage rather than weakness • Remember: "Our strengths are our vulnerabilities" is one of life's profound paradoxes
Release the Weight of Others' Expectations	Freedom comes from defining success on your own terms.	• Recognize when you're carrying burdens or expectations that aren't yours • Practice discernment about which societal expectations actually align with your values • Release the need to

Core Principle	Description	Practical Applications
		shape yourself according to others' molds • Understand that authentic power comes from defining success on your own terms • Remember: "We can only move forwards and upwards when we're in synchronicity with ourselves"
Develop Emotional Intelligence Through Self-Reflection	Understanding your emotional patterns leads to wiser choices.	• Build awareness of how your emotions influence your decisions and relationships • Practice recognizing emotional patterns in your daily interactions • Develop empathy for yourself and others through understanding emotional roots • Learn to translate emotional signals into practical wisdom • Remember: Emotional intelligence begins with your relationship with yourself

II.   ABOUT THE AUTHOR

A truth seeker committed to living an authentic life, I've navigated a transformative path guided by dignity, honesty, and self-awareness. Born in Bulgaria in 1982, I journeyed through South Africa in my teens before finding home in Australia by the end of 2023. As a commercial and intellectual property lawyer licensed in South Africa and Australia, I blend a dynamic professional career with a profound commitment to personal growth. My journey began by confronting internalized expectations and untrue belief systems that once constrained my spirit. Through deep introspection, I discovered the transformative power of self-awareness and emotional clarity, uncovering a path to personal empowerment that now defines my professional and personal mission.

Embracing multiple roles - a wife, mother to two daughters, sister, daughter, and friend - I've learned to cherish the connections that illuminate my path. Driven by a passionate commitment to personal transformation, I strive to offer guidance to those who wish to break free from limiting beliefs and emotional stagnation. Through my writing and work, I aim to be a beacon of hope for those ready to reclaim their truth, transcend past constraints, and step into a life of profound clarity, presence, and fulfillment.

III.   ACKNOWLEDGEMENTS

Creating this book has been a transformative journey, made possible by the incredible people who supported me along the way.

A heartfelt thank you to Alex Woodburne for the beautiful cover design, and to Carla de Klerk for bringing the book's visual essence to life.

To my dear friends Alexis Apostolidis and Karansingth Kapitan - two extraordinary souls who have been crucial to this journey. Alexis, with your legal genius and wit that keeps me laughing and thinking in equal measure, and Karan, a wise, intentional, spiritually evolved, intelligent human who selflessly supports me on my path, your contributions have been invaluable.

Gerhard Pretorius, your wisdom and guidance through my personal journey of growth have been profound. You are amazing!

To my husband, whose support and understanding have been my foundation - thank you for giving me the freedom to fully dedicate myself to this project.

I am grateful for every experience, challenge, and connection that has allowed me to break free from limiting beliefs and step into my truest self. This book is a testament to that journey.

264

Thank you to each person who has been part of bringing Chasing Footnotes to life.